UNDERTOW

UNDERTOW

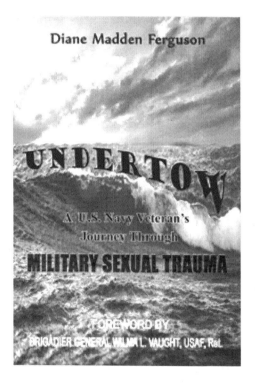

Copyright © 2016 by the Author,
Diane Madden Ferguson

Undertow

FIRST EDITION

Undertow is written and self-published by the author,
Diane Madden Ferguson.

Cover Design by Diane Ferguson and Jennifer Sweete
Cover Art Graphic Design by Jennifer Sweete

Edited by Jennifer Sweete with author
Interior Design & Layout by Jennifer Sweete

Hard Cover
13 ISBN: 978-0-9982647-1-4
10 ISBN: 0-9982647-1-7

Soft Cover
13 ISBN: 978-0-9982647-0-7
10 ISBN: 0-9982647-0-9

DEDICATION

To all those who had a genuine desire to serve our country
but came to know the horrors of

Military Sexual Trauma

- ❖ Know you are not alone
- ❖ Your journey home awaits
- ❖ May your heart be healed
- ❖ May your soul find peace
- ❖ May you find your voice

ACKNOWLEDGMENTS

A lifetime of thanks to those who have loved me while never knowing of my wounded heart and soul. Your unconditional love and understanding has carried me through the darkness; the joy and light of each of you has filled my life. You have brought me courage in the writing of this book.

To each female who ever tried and failed to be my friend, I acknowledge my part in the conflicts and pain, and forgive fate for our final partings. Blessed be the female friends who rose to the challenge of bonding with me—redheads and non-redheads alike—I know it wasn't always easy. You brought me such support of my spirit in the writing of this book.

To the men who are truly at the very core of the foundation of my life, I cherish your character, your integrity, and your authenticity. You are the men who have unknowingly slain many of my demons over the years just by being the men that you are. It is from you that I drew hope and perseverance in the writing of this book.

To my accountability partner, Bobbi. You've always had my back. You keep me grounded. You call me out and kick my ass, when necessary. You know the direction of my heart and thoughts often before I do. It's your unwavering voice of empathy and bond of compassionate friendship that has cradled and bolstered me through the process of writing this book.

With the sincerest thanks from my heart, I acknowledge the sound counsel and wisdom infused in my journey by my VetCenter therapists. I am no longer afraid, without purpose and direction. With your guidance and support, I have found my voice and encouragement to face MST with a new awareness and perspective.

Grateful appreciation to my initial editorial review board for your contributions in the beginning stages of bringing the telling of my story to life. Thank you all.

I would be remiss if I didn't acknowledge the rescue efforts of my editor and graphic designer, Jennifer Sweete. I was adrift—virtually lost at sea. Together we brought this ship into the shore. Attaboys all around!

I am honored and humbled by Brigadier General Wilma Vaught's heartfelt contribution to the Foreword for this book. The impact of her words from a caring heart fortified my resolve. I am beyond grateful and I thank you.

Most importantly, I acknowledge **ME** in the writing of this book. In acknowledging all of you here, I realize I am gathering the fragments of my own being back into wholeness. I have now found my courage, my support system, my champions, my strengths, my hope, my perseverance and resilience, and **MY VOICE.**

I WILL NOT GIVE UP.

I WILL NOT GIVE IN.

I WILL GIVE IT ALL I'VE GOT!

TABLE OF CONTENTS

FOREWORD

BY

BRIGADIER GENERAL
WILMA L. VAUGHT USAF, Ret.

Because of my career, I have come to know and care about a lot of women veterans. I write from the perspective of a woman veteran with more than 28 years of military service and as the nearly three-decades-long President of the Women in Military Service for America Memorial Foundation (WIMSA). The Foundation's original mission was to build a memorial honoring all our servicewomen. Today, and perhaps more importantly, the Foundation and Memorial provide a forum for collecting and telling the story of women's service to our nation.

Sadly, during those some 60 years, I've listened to many stories about incidents of military sexual assault and abuse, read countless news articles, and endeavored to help when I could. In recent years, a number of books have been written by women suffering from sexual assault and its aftermath, as well as those by numerous authors concerned about this serious problem in our military, on our college campuses, and throughout our society.

Diane Ferguson told me she had hidden her story of military assault and abuse from her family and friends for some 40 years. And, for as many years, she suffered devastating, physical, mental and emotional trauma. Now she wants to alert women, particularly young women, to the dangers of a permissive military environment that she believes continues to exist today. Her purpose is to help women avoid military sexual assault and abuse and the trauma that comes with it. So compelling was her 40-year journey, I had to step up too by writing this Foreword.

It's hard to come to terms with how your fellow servicemembers —your battle buddies—those you consider friends and can trust, are anything but. That was Diane's experience in the 1970s. Despite the years of work by many members of Congress (primarily women), along with the diligent efforts of the Department of Defense and the military services to attack this problem and stop it, military sexual assault and abuse continues to persist. Our job is to keep up the pressure and to not give up. Our military, our treasured sons and daughters, and future generations of Americans deserve no less.

There is so much I'd like to say about this story but it's Diane's story. I'm compelled, however, to say that you will seldom read another story of anyone, particularly of those who were in a situation like hers, who gave more of her life trying to do the right thing for her country and to do her job in the face of heinous abuse. She has suffered physically, mentally and emotionally. To me, she is a hero!

Wilma Vaught

Brigadier General Wilma L. Vaught, USAFR is a retired American military leader. She was the first woman to deploy with an Air Force bomber unit, and the first woman to reach the rank of Brigadier General from the comptroller field.

PREFACE

How will I relate to the little girl I once was and have left behind? So many promises made as yet unkept. I am taking steps to restore her. It is those steps of healing I am counting on to fulfill my promises made to her over the many years and the sharing of the secrets we kept.

She is always with me yet I keep her at a distance. We know we are alone in this. For her own safety I insulate her, still keeping care she isn't destroyed by all we endured through those five abusive years in the military. As for the years since, there is a sorrow to the repeating question, "What would you have had me do differently back then?" Followed by the hollow cry coming from within, "What would you have me do now?"

What happened to me while enlisted in the US Navy, I have corralled into a safe harbor to give myself enough emotional distance to manage the memories of my life as it was during those five years. These are my thoughts, my memories, and the metaphors I've come to use to describe my experiences.

The undertow of the sea churns up debris, disorienting and forcefully tumbling the current before settling the waves to a predictable pattern or rhythm until the next cycle begins. A single wave on the sea will become altered in its intensity, duration, strength, and direction under the control of the undertow. How resilient will the wave be when pulled into the undertow—this time or the next, or each time after that? How much pulling and pushing and crashing against the rocks can one person endure?

I found myself constantly drawn back to the water, to the ocean, to the rhythmic pulsations of the waves as if the answer I so desperately hoped for would wash ashore—thinking this only made good sense because I *was* a WAVE.

When I watched the waves push toward the shore and ebb back out to sea, I'd be gently mesmerized by the constant motion—ebb and flow—consistently predictable yet each wave completely unique in its form and force.

What happened on the surface gracefully hid what churned below the violent undertow. I imagined only I knew the messages in the waves. And so it was: the undertow, my sanctuary and my nemesis. As I felt the undertow wash over me and pull me down, how easy it would have been to yield in utter collapse. The stronger pull for me, however, was hearing the little girl whisper, "You promised me. You promised me." Knowing I had not fulfilled even the smallest of the many promises I made to her gave me the strength to overpower any thought of submission. Her sad little voice would plead with me to find the strength to carry on for both of us.

The riptide was vanquished . . . for the moment. I dug deeper into my reserve of resilience. It wasn't a character trait so strong as tenacity, perseverance, or even resilience, per se. It was a softer, more loving commitment, a tender promise made to a trusting young girl. It was a promise made too many times in the aftermath of far too many traumatic assaults. A promise meant to be kept, heartfelt and directly from my soul, which steadied my resolve. A promise, not of fear, shame or even weakness, but rather one of preservation in hopes of one day when validation would come. A promise of one day when those in power would listen and we would finally be heard.

Our bond would not be shredded by the undertow. The force that pulled us under also propelled us back into the sanctuary of hope. For all the empty promises of a life so well-intentioned, we knew the only trust to be believed was ours within.

The lasting effects of MST (Military Sexual Trauma) are not unlike the undertow. It does not have to dictate or define the life of a young wave. A single wave on the sea will feel the impact; however, the ebb and flow of tide and time will be reckoned with and ultimately reconciled.

The commitment to serve my country could not be diminished by the well-established, testosterone-infused culture of such long accepted and damaging behaviors. Nor would 40 years erase the horrors of my memories.

For many years, the military environment had demonstratively shown itself to be unchanged. Blaming the victimized and showing tolerance (and even support) to the predators gave the appearance of being the Navy's M.O. for addressing men's unhealthy, perverse behaviors.

This isn't just a Navy flaw. This problem goes as far back as the Eisenhower administration, when the president ordered a congressional investigation of the slander campaign against US Army servicewomen, the source of which was revealed to be both officers and enlisted US Army servicemen. In an effort to defame and dishonor women in the US Army, WACs' uniforms were sold by servicemen to prostitutes who wore them while openly soliciting sex, much to the denigration of the women in actual military service. To Eisenhower's credit, the moment he learned of this behavior he ensured the immediate end of it.

Attitudes in the Navy passively allowed such various behaviors of nefarious lawlessness and unwavering tolerance that gave an unspoken permission and encouragement of these types of unconscionable attitudes and behaviors of Naval servicemen. Cloaked as just another good story to share with their shipmates left these despicable behaviors looked upon as just part of the daily routine and a rite of passage.

The group mentality of the Master-at-Arms on the leeward side of GITMO (Guantánamo Bay) to construct, collaborate and conceal a truly horrific scenario upon a young WAVE away from home for the first time and new to the Navy went beyond the abuse of legal authority and trust. It went far beyond poor judgment or bad character. I am still trying to make sense of what happened to me.

No matter what the MST caused in my life, it was my choice to make a life better in my resilience to seek out the positives in my service to our country. Back in the 1970s, no one would have listened even if I had found the strength to levy charges. What happened was simply the price of being allowed into the boys club.

The horrors of MST robbed me of my ability to trust, and the collateral damage was my innocence. The horrors were not going to rob me of honor and duty. I could only save myself by the forbearance of the pain. It did not make me a victim. It made me a survivor. Those unknown to me who were aware of my experiences respected me for maintaining a professional demeanor. It was noted in my various performance evaluations that I demonstrated I was able to "carry on admirably regardless of personal tragedy." I foolishly believed no one knew the absolute truth of my struggles. Yet remarks such as these recurred frequently throughout my evaluations, leaving me to believe otherwise now.

Even though I could feel the tugging and pulling at my spirit, I clearly remember how determined I was to maintain pride in my contribution to our country, along with my resolve not to allow my spirit to become enveloped by the undertow.

What concerns me most about this journey is the fractured references I make to myself in my thoughts and in the telling of what happened. I never identify as just "me." I say "my" or "her" or "the single wave" and "the little girl." I never just say "**me**." I find it helps to detach from some moments and take ownership of others. I need to heal the fracture. I need to own the MST fully and celebrate my refusal to let it destroy me. I need to forgive myself for being so naïve at having allowed myself to be so taken in. I didn't knowingly leave myself open, but I wasn't vigilant in preventing it either. I am angry with myself for being so ignorant of the danger. I need to forgive myself. And, I need to warn others.

I choose free will to make this decision to fight off the wretched emptiness the MST brought to my life. My time in the US Navy was not all bad. I will *not* allow the MST to tarnish the good I did and any happy memories I made during that time. I served with honor and integrity. I went on to build a life after the Navy, while continuing to serve my community with honor and integrity. My life is solid and more than I could ever have hoped or imagined. I am blessed to have survived MST, but I know I am severely wounded. It is time to end the secrecy that has been heart-wrenching and caused me so much loneliness. Time has shown itself to me.

Expect no grand literary references going forward.

Simple truths from a tender heart will make reference to the trauma in cautious measure.

Entering the US Navy, my heart soared just before it crashed to the ground. Feelings so long tucked away, or more truthfully locked away, will be given freedom of expression in their sharing. More certain in the offering is the realization that no such candor should need to be censored. Though it never should've happened in the first place, here we are. It did happen and continues to happen to others even as I write this book.

It has been pure self-indulgence to imagine no one feeling so deeply and sincerely as I. Whether whimsy or folly, my present, exposed sadness at the loss of my innocence drives me forward. For so long my anger has been my armor. These painful experiences were real when only I knew of them. Once shared, they seem almost *surreal*. My very hopes and aspirations that once vanished like a wisp of fog in the wind are now changing into something new and beautiful.

It will not be the undertow that takes my last breath. It will be the truth of the long kept promises being fulfilled. No secrets will be kept. They, too, have been quiet far too long. Five years of military sexual trauma, buried under 40 more will not be short in the telling.

Please take this journey with me through the ugliness of posttraumatic stress disorder (PTSD). I shoved the pain down deep. I promised the wounded little girl inside me that one day we would face the horror, the pain, and the agony of what was done to me/us. I promised the little girl we would have an admirable and respectable life that was not defined by our victimization—a life full of love and success.

One day when the time was right, we would expose it all—names, dates and locations. We would make those in authority listen. We would warn the other young girls. We would feel sad for the ones we couldn't warn in time to prevent their MST. We had to wait for the right moment in time to keep the promises we made and share the secrets we kept.

40 years now passed. I spoke to no one of this before now, but for the little girl in pain within me. Not my husband. Not my children. Not my parents or my brothers. Not even the

dearest of my friends. I could have, but to what end? What good could come from them knowing? It would only hurt them in a way I could not verbalize even for myself.

The wait for the right moment is over. The moment is now. Perhaps it's the luxury of my age in knowing my life is more behind me than it is ahead of me. It's an oddly comforting thought. Life becomes more about keeping promises than keeping secrets.

Dear reader, it is about to get ugly in a graphically shared, heart-wrenching, first-person accounting of Military Sexual Trauma.

I ask you to be brave as you read on. Allow yourself to set this book down and come back to it when you find you can take on a bit more of the telling. Find the courage to read on. Cry. Get angry. Be outraged, but not for me alone—for so many.

Please take this journey with me and pray the journey keeps you or a loved one safe from harm.

FLAWED

I count in a whisper the dreams I held dear

I catch myself wishing and holding in fear

I promise myself I will not shed a tear

I swallow the lump as I let my throat clear

I cautiously wait as I quietly listen

If my tears leave my eyes, my secrets will glisten

If my tears leave my eyes, who'll be there to kiss them?

If my tears leave my eyes, will anyone miss them?

Now please tell me, who will hold me

for all the lies that they told me?

The world is going to know what I've tried to conceal

It leaves me to wonder - was this at all real?

My tears aren't for sharing; my thoughts are my own

I love to be loved, but still be alone

I cherish my peace; my contented repose

I'm guarded and selfish of what anyone knows

"Flawed" © Diane Madden Ferguson

Chapter One
By Way of Explanation

Memories are funny things. They imprint themselves almost randomly in our minds. Memories allow us to remember some things with little effort and yet deny us access to other things we want to remember.

Every word I share in this telling is fully accurate to the best of my recollection. I easily remember the names of those who were kind to me but cannot always recall the names of those who harmed me so deeply.

Some of the names that I initially couldn't recall came to me at odd times over the course of writing this book. When my soul had quieted my darker thoughts, a previously lost name would be released into my memory like a candy placed on my pillow. It gave me comfort. It also sent me back to my writing to revise it to include the name.

I have shared my timeline of duty stations, my assignments and the dates assigned there, along with the names I share, both truthfully and accurately. Anyone stationed with me or who knew me back then will have little doubt of whom I'm speaking.

Some of the names I have altered because I don't want to feed their egos by letting them see their names in print. Other names will be the real names with my thanks for their kindness. I want you to know there were good and admirable men who passed through my naval career. Admittedly, each horrendous encounter began with me believing a particular person to be good and honorable. It was only after being attacked or raped by that person that I would discover how wrong I had been.

There are gaps in the telling. I refuse to fabricate events to reweave the narrative into a comfortable continuity. There is no piece of fiction in my book. I will bring you along on my journey, following my path as I walked it. There is a difference between a biography and a memoir. This is a bit of both. It is

1

the sadly truthful story of a young girl who became victim of her own innocence in a culture she was ill prepared to fend off. I view the gaps and the denied memories as my psyche's gift to my heart. Maybe I'm not strong enough to remember anything more than I have. I will share with you only what I remember, and will not provide "fillers" to try to make sense of what happened.

Oddly, I still feel the need to explain myself to the people of my hometown and those who knew me growing up. (We survivors are constantly becoming aware of new topics to share with our counselors. Hmmm.)

As for me not telling anyone in West Chicago prior to this, I now offer this explanation. I wasn't going to let the attacks define me and add grist to the rumor mill in my little hometown. This was most clearly defined for me when I was raped in my apartment just two blocks from where the West Chicago Police Department is currently located and six blocks from where my brother lived at that time. I would have resented the whispers, the pity, or the blame-placing. I did not want my brother to be ashamed for me, or feel responsible in any way from that experience—not then, not now. My silence was born of my refusal to allow anyone to know of or react to this lest my identity as a person or the value of my military service be labeled in a context unacceptable to me.

As it was, I had garnered respect and admiration for my service and later for my educational achievements and professional successes. "Hometown Girl Makes Good!" I liked that label. I'd earned it. I was not then nor am I now willing to have any of the MST destroy me.

There will be some who won't believe or perhaps relate to my story. They have my understanding. I thank them for buying or borrowing this book and giving it a try. I would hope they would pass it on to someone who might understand and find solace in knowing they are not alone. Unfortunately, disbelief itself fosters the horrific environment of MST to continue to exist.

Believe it! Wake up! Get angry! Be outraged!

To those who wish I'd told you sooner or had chosen you to confide in, please accept my apology. Know in your heart that at the time I simply couldn't, and forgive me my painful choices. My inner spirit prompted the order of when and whom I told. A whisper telling me that a certain person in a certain moment was safe to confide in. Does it make any sense our daughter was the very first one I told? Actually, it does if you're aware of the special bond she and I share. She carries my mother's courage in her very soul and perhaps channeled my mother's spirit the day I found the words to share my story.

To those who find themselves wondering about this order of revelation, I don't fully understand it myself. It's neither here nor there. But, one by one, I told those closest to me before the book went to print. Oddly enough, to my relief and surprise (yet I shouldn't be surprised at all because they love me beyond measure) the telling cleared up more confusion than it created. No one went "POOF" and disappeared.

Every one of them refused to entertain any notion of me falling short of being a good mom. Anytime I would express doubts I was met with completely opposing statements such as, "Stop right there. You were a great mom." Every Leo (as in the lion of the zodiac) in my life said almost exactly the same thing. Hearing this was all the more meaningful, absolutely the most meaningful when spoken by my firstborn, our son. After being told by Navy medical personnel that I'd not be able to have children as a result of what had been done to me as their lab rat (i.e., part of their clinical trials), my son is my miracle. Then. Today. Always.

As I sit here now at age 63 and reflect on my life as one full of blessings yet also too many secrets kept and too many promises not, I hope with all my heart that your journey through this narrative will explain everything at last.

Chapter Two
What Was I Thinking

In retrospect, I can say, "What was I thinking?" in bewilderment, considering the outcome. What I was thinking the day I signed my enlistment papers held so much more wholesome intention than the outcome yielded.

I was 20 years old in 1973. My hometown was still recovering from the '60s. The remnants of that free-love decade didn't leave me with many viable options. Everywhere I looked, the choices weren't great. I had one boyfriend the last two years of high school and the two years following graduation. He drank. He beat me. He had me nearly convinced he was the best offer I'd ever hope to get. I almost believed him. I knew a life with him would end badly but I believed I didn't have many options.

As frightened of the future as I was, I knew I wanted to get out of town. I had a job not worth having. My parents' 25th wedding anniversary was coming up. I found it sad that I couldn't afford even so much as a card to give them. For all the life-lessons they'd taught me and my brothers—some good, some tragic—I felt just a card wouldn't be enough even if I could afford one.

Admittedly, our family dynamic was far less than perfect. Suffice to say it was pretty messed up. Let me be clear. It was no episode of Ozzie and Harriet. Ward and June Cleaver did not live next door. Donna Reed, Ricky Nelson and Fred McMurray were not from the neighborhood.

We reach a point in our lives where we have to forgive our parents for being human. Very likely, they once had hopes and dreams that faded away as parenthood and life sucked them into their shortcomings. I have long since found that point of forgiveness for my parents. While they may not have been the best choice for each other, they raised strong, independent, decent children who grew up to be kind, respectful and honest adults.

My oldest brother died in a car crash in 1968. My next oldest brother was married in 1969 and still is to this day. He was building a strong, loving family environment worthy of respect in spite of our difficult upbringing. He worked hard to achieve the life he and his family have now. My third in birth order and peacemaker brother had joined the US Navy in 1970 with plans to make it a career, which he did for 23 years.

So what was I thinking? My thoughts were scattered at best. I never wanted to run from my life. I wanted to run to a new life, one I could be proud to have lived.

I was contributing nothing to the world by remaining in West Chicago. I was academically gifted, although most often chose not to use my intellect for the best of purposes. As was once pointed out to me by one of my brothers, I was, basically, a "fuck up" at life. The remark might have seemed hurtful but for the fact that I agreed.

The summation was not at all what I wanted as my legacy. With no decent job and no ability to go to college, I realized not being able to buy an anniversary card for my folks was the least of my worries.

What was I thinking? If I presented my parents with my enlistment papers then I could go into the military and with one simple commitment make them more proud of me than they ever had been. My brothers would and did respect my very adult decision. I could and did unload the abusive boyfriend. I could and did have an opportunity to attend college, *and* I earned my Master's degree in 2010, with honors.

As frightened as I was at the onset of this decision, the overwhelming sense of pride to be serving my country was stronger than my fear. Once I finally decided to enlist in the Navy everything else took on a newfound clarity—not just of thought but also understanding my purpose. Finally, my life took on a new direction.

Every sense of my life—the sights, the smells, the sounds of West Chicago—came alive with a new awareness. All the beautiful trees in town seem to rustle their leaves for me as if saying goodbye. Breezes smelled sweeter. The grass seemed more lush—not just the smoke of it wafting from the head-shop on Arbor Avenue, but the carpets of well-manicured lawns around town. It's like I was seeing my hometown for the first time, but the emotional embrace was one of farewell.

Every reaction I anticipated from my family was just as I'd hoped. My father, a former Army Air Corps officer and Purdue alumni, cried and said, "You'll be fine baby. You go show 'em." My mother cried even more as she said, "Give them hell, baby! Let them know you were there!"

So it was to be in 1973. I was going to grab onto my life by serving my country in the United States Navy. Consumed in thought, the drive into Chicago to the induction center was unremarkable. The reality set in when the Marine Corps officer barked out, "Attention! Raise your right hand! Repeat after me." The grace of purpose really settled over me like a cloak warmed in front of the fire. As I spoke the words in response to the order, my voice did not tremble. My determination was unwavering. I was proud to have sworn to protect and defend my country. It was the single most solemn moment of my life. It was without hesitation. No doubt in my conviction. I would make good on my word. I was never more sure of anything in my life.

On my parents' 25th wedding anniversary, May 17, 1973, I officially belonged to the United States Navy. Boot camp would wait until June. Time to say goodbye to We-Go (West Chicago). My last day at work at the Tumble Inn, the entire bar stood and sang "Anchors Aweigh" when I walked in. It meant so much to me. What a great send-off!

With my fresh-faced innocence, I left my small hometown. I was full of dreams and aspirations, and a genuine desire to serve my country. I often thought back on my parents' words and tears when I needed to refocus my motivation to serve my country with honor and dignity.

I can remember my annoyance and confusion on my 18th birthday when I went to the post office to register for the draft. It was only then that I found out that females don't do that. I was frustrated. My father was amused. I didn't know then that we would revisit my potential military career just a few short years later.

My father's military career was a highly decorated one. We were raised on his stories of duty, honor, and country—all values that were mainstream in the '50s. With my two oldest brothers enlisted in the United States Air Force and my brother Neil and I enlisted in the Navy, I am proud to report that not one of us had waited to be drafted.

Not too very long into my active duty in the Navy, I fell victim to my naïvety. I steadfastly refused to relinquish my dignity. My duty to country became one of resilience. My tenacious commitment became my armor. Without sharing too many details, let me just say that my childhood prepared me with a strong foundation of character to withstand the damage I would sustain in the months and years ahead.

In a barrage of sexual attacks that took place during my five years of Navy experience to follow, I gathered every ounce of military bearing within me. Refusing to allow the brutality to define or destroy my career or my spirit, I was determined to serve with honor. I would not return home in disgrace.

What I was thinking the day I enlisted, and remembering my parents' tears (or maybe their fears) was far different from my thoughts the day I was discharged. But those thoughts, culminating on March 30, 1978, would stoically stay my own for nearly 40 years longer. Until now.

Chapter Three
Forewarned is Forearmed

Just as the lay of the land is forever changing, so the laws of the land change as well. Forewarned is forearmed and I was neither. The following incidents and occurrences are as much for my telling as they are for those who might read and be better armed for a safer and saner experience in the military and the battlefield of life in general.

Military Sexual Trauma (MST) permeates the ranks as an insidious fact of the armed forces. As defined by the Center for Deployment Psychology, Military Sexual Trauma (MST) is an experience, not a diagnosis. It is a phrase that was coined by the Department of Veterans Affairs, not by the Department of Defense.

MST is distinctively inflicted upon a service member of the military by a fellow soldier, officer, or other military affiliate. The violation of this military bond of brotherhood makes MST all the more overwhelmingly abhorrent and irreconcilable. It is akin to incest.

Victims of MST tend to keep the horrors of these tragedies to themselves and are six times more likely to commit suicide than a combat veteran.

So many uniformed women of our armed forces are isolated by these painful and agonizing experiences as they adopt a "suffer in silence" stance. The violated become exceptionally adept at concealing their trauma—and it becomes a festering wound.

I kept quiet nearly 40 years while promising myself to someday expose the horrors of my personal experience with MST. Knowing that predators still await their victims, I can no longer remain silent.

Congressional mandates, military tribunals, Pentagon investigations and statistics, and military awareness programs that blame the victims for the attack, all have fallen severely short of the mark in correcting this wrong. Military Sexual Trauma will continue until and unless good and decent Americans become aware and outraged. Only then is there hope it will cease.

Attention to this problem has been building for some time. In January 2011, a reporter for *Newsweek Magazine* published an article titled "Judge Dismisses Epidemic of Rape in Military Case," stating that "Women are more likely to be assaulted by a fellow soldier than killed in combat."

In December 2012, the *American Foreign Press* reported that during a one-year period between 2010 and 2011, the Pentagon received 3,192 reports of assaults. This figure is approximately 20% of those that actually occurred, the rest going unreported most often due to fear of retaliation. When viewed from the full percentage this equates to approximately 44 assaults per day.

In the 2012 documentary titled *The Invisible War*—a Sundance Award winner—data is brought forth substantiating that in the past 25 years more than 500,000 people, mostly women by percentage, have been sexually assaulted while serving in the United States armed forces.

In September 2013, Congress received the US Commission on Civil Rights, 2013 Statutory Report on Sexual Assault in the Military. That 2012 fiscal year report included the results of an anonymous survey of military personnel that stated 1 in 4 females confidentially admitted being sexually assaulted while serving in the military, although only 34% of those females officially reported the assault.

On June 9, 2016, after nearly a decade of determined efforts by Senator Kirsten Gillibrand of New York, the Senate passed the Military Justice Improvement Act (MJIA). The MJIA removes the ability of the military chain of command to manipulate, hide, and bury military sexual assault. MJIA assures that a completely separate branch of trained prosecutors within the military bypasses the authority and reach of the military chain of command.

MJIA assures this special legal branch of the military now handles *all* military sexual assaults; thereby moving the direct reporting of such assaults and judicial outcomes to a higher, autonomous authority, ensuring sexual predators are punished. As a result, the hope is that the ongoing climate that allowed retaliation against survivors of MST who dared to report it will be brought to a resounding end.

Ironically, on the heels of the Senate passing the MJIA, a mere five days later the Senate went on to pass the $602 billion Defense Authorization Bill/Act (NDAA) that included a requirement for women turning 18 on or after January 1, 2018 to register for Selective Service (i.e., the "draft").

With more women entering the military than ever before and now being ushered toward the military draft, a new day is definitely dawning. Who will protect and serve those who protect and serve?

Chapter Four
Chronicle of Incidents and Occurrences

The following "Incidents" are word-for-word as I filed them with the Veterans Administration—with a few minor editorial adjustments in brackets to benefit the reader. For the writing of this book, most of the names have been replaced by fictitious initials or nicknames to protect the innocent as well as the guilty (as much as I would like to scream their names from the rooftops for all to hear).

Commander Alvin Marsh and my brother, Neil, retain their real names in this book for they are of the highest caliber of integrity and compassion, and have granted me permission to use their names in print.

My claims were deemed founded by the Veterans Administration, which entitled me to receive some disability benefits from the VA. Following the VA's findings and final decision, these same incidents were then the basis for my Social Security disability claim.

The "Odd Occurrences" I am including are my personal experiences as I remember them. I will share them to the best of my ability and recollection.

Deep breath . . . the journey begins . . .

Incident #1
9 Jan 74 to 21 Jul 74 - GITMO Tour

It was my first time out of the United States. Guantanamo Bay, Cuba was my first real duty station following my "A" school at Great Lakes. I was 20 years old and very much looking forward to a career in the Navy.

GITMO was considered isolated duty—one-year tour. Being on isolated duty prevents sailors from bringing their spouses and families for the year but a commitment to two years allowed relocation of family for the core 12 months of the assignment. This left many married men temporarily unattached or unsupervised. Women sailors were not allowed a two-year commitment and therefore could never bring family.

There were approximately 75-80 females assigned to the entire base; both leeward and windward sides of the bay. We females arrived in "broods" of five or six at a time. [A group of] 17 males met our [brood] and took us to dinner the night we arrived. I wondered how they got the lucky assignment or if it was their turn in the rotation. There were approximately 2000-3000 male sailors in GITMO with the population fluctuating as our naval vessels and those of "friendly" countries passed through the training area.

All female sailors were housed on the windward side of the bay at the Gold Hill Barracks. My first assignment was mess hall cleanup duty on the leeward side of the bay. We were required to ride the ferry to and from the chow hall—a brief 20-minute crossing of the bay with many others having similar logistical obligations. We were permitted to enjoy both the leeward and windward side facilities and activities while off-duty as well. The ferry left the windward side on the hour and left the leeward side of the bay on the half hour.

We were cautioned to keep our wits about us as females. We were not to travel alone to the beach, to the stables, to the pools, etc. but always be in groups due to the risks to our personal safety while on isolated duty. We were told of the Cubans who did day-work on the base and the Jamaicans who lived on the base. We were to report even the smallest of infractions.

I followed the directive. I was happy to be befriended by the Aviation Ordinance Division as their "little sister"—something like being designated a fraternity's kid sister. I felt it added another layer to my personal protection. I knew they would keep me safe; advise me on Navy life and just generally watch over me until my older brother Neil (an air-traffic controller) joined me in March for brother/sister duty. I gained confidence in my ability to judge good character. I had become overconfident in my surroundings and I let my guard down.

14 Jan 74, 2100hrs. While on the ferry back to the windward side, I was approached by a male Jamaican civilian who graphically propositioned me several times during the crossing. He suggested sexual acts I had never heard of and professed his skills at rendering a young woman exhausted. I was trapped for the entire crossing, I'd move away and he'd see it as a ploy and tease. There was no getting away. But the ferry landed and I boarded the Navy bus and escaped him.

I became physically ill overnight thinking of the vile behavior of the Jamaican. I checked in at sick call to report being accosted as we had been instructed. The medical staff noted my illness in my record as "Nervous Condition" and "Situational Stress Reaction." I was given a huge dose of Valium and Dalman (I don't know what that was, maybe for the vomiting).

I was told to report the incident to the Master-at-Arms (MAA) on the duty side (Leeward) where I'd boarded the ferry and to "be more careful - toughen up." I didn't consider it anything more than a learning experience caused by my own lax behavior. I needed to be more aware of my surroundings.

I went to the MAA on leeward side—the base police. I reported the incident. I was assured the Jamaican would be dealt with Navy style. I became friendly with the whole MAA attachment. My own godfather was a cop back home and had been in the Navy. I saw another layer of protection in the association. No harm really. Live and learn.

I really was enjoying my Navy life. I was young and single. I had all the hopes and dreams of my career ahead of me. I was about to turn 21 years old. I'm in Cuba. My party is going to be on the beach on a tropical island. My memory bucket would overflow with a 21st birthday no one would forget.

There was such a sense of family, love and acceptance as anyone and everyone was invited to my party. The resourceful gift-giving offerings were hilarious. With no duty tax, bottles of rum were 25-50¢ and almost everyone brought me a bottle. The mess crew cooked up over 200 pieces of chicken. The Spud locker produce team made gallon buckets of all sorts of salads. My birthday cake was made by the Baker's team. Every guy who'd brought his guitar to Cuba with him came to the party and sang and played. There was a Marine on Conga drums and a Navy Seal with bongos.

Non-stop laughter and bonfires filled the air—this is my new family. I was safe. I felt loved. We had secured our bonfire party permit so we were cleared to be on

13

the beach. It was a Navy blowout for the record books. Only about 25 or so of the 83 females on base attended. It was okay but they were going to miss the really great time.

Then it was time for "the birthday gauntlet." I was given a choice of 1) fun, 2) a bit more fun, and 3) raunchy. I asked what Option 2 involved. I wanted a concrete definition of fun. The self-proclaimed Master of Ceremonies, one of the Chiefs from the mess hall said that fun would be defined by me, the birthday girl. The two levels of fun were hugs and kisses or birthday spankings. My call. My idea of fun.

I turned to look at the gauntlet to assess before making my choice. Oh, my! There were upwards of 150 to 200 guys awaiting my approach. I opted for hugs and kisses as I turned to face my subjects. As I ascended my path to the gauntlet, I was thinking *I love my Navy life!*

My Navy life—work hard, serve my country and have the time of my life. I made a valiant effort to progress down the gauntlet. All shapes, sizes, colors, and ethnicities of beautiful sculpted, healthy all-American males stood ready to kiss me on my 21st birthday. We also had three British sailors from the HMS Bon Homme Richard, which was moored in the Bay for training. The Brits thought they would join us for an American birthday party. Lucky me!

I made it through the birthday kisses and hugs. I got all manner of kisses. My hand was kissed while someone bowed before me. The cheeks of my face also, as was my forehead. My feet were graced with kisses. My cleavage was lovingly kissed by a Navy SEAL with a tenderness not usually associated with a trained killer. I admit I was afraid not to let him kiss his chosen spot. No one touched me, or groped me or grabbed me. It was all in fun. There was so much laughter as I was spun and twirled and passed down the gauntlet with my feet hardly touching the ground. It was not a precursor to the Tailhook scandal. It was done with style and class. It was playful.

Memories of my 21st birthday will make me smile long into my eighties as I rock away on my front porch. I didn't make it through the entire gauntlet before I hyperventilated. My female battalion of party attendees picked up the slack where I left off and finished off my birthday gauntlet; or tried. I sat laughing, watching those I'd already kissed run to the end of the gauntlet to form up for more. It went on forever, so it seemed. It was hilarious. I was so happy I had found this new life.

In stark contrast, barreling across the beach came two USMC trucks loaded with *the few, the proud,* the party crashers. At first, we thought they were just making an entrance because they were fashionably late. The severity of the situation

14

snapped us back to reality. The Marines were forcibly removing us from the beach. I was literally picked up by my waistband and thrown eight feet into the back of the transport vehicle.

The Marine looked at me with a stone cold gaze and said, "Hey Dorothy! You're not in fucking Kansas anymore!" He pointed to the fence line and snarled, "Those are Castro's tanks! They are running the fence line because of your little birthday party."

It foreshadowed the other realities I would need to face up to in the months ahead.

Life settled back into a comfortable routine of taking the ferry over Guantanamo Bay to work, comings back to the barracks on the ferry, going to the chow hall, returning to barracks, and going to bed and get up and doing it all over again. Seven days a week. Duty. Service. Country. I had never worked so hard or learned so much so quickly, or been so tired in my life. I was loving it.

I hadn't really given much thought to the incident with the Jamaican on the ferry. I had put it behind me. Something good had come out of it. I'd made friends with some of the base police around the leeward side of the island. So I was comfortable stopping in to say hello when I finished up the mess hall before catching ferry back over to the barracks.

After reporting the incident from the ferry to the MAA, a few weeks later, I met "D". He was a career Navy man (18 years) from Cameron, West Virginia. He was a Boiler Tech 1st Class assigned to Base Police as a Master-at-Arms. It sickens me to think of him at all so it's harder now to recall what it was about him that I found appealing. It hurts to know I ever found him attractive but he had stolen my heart and my innocence with it.

He was 17 years older than me. It wasn't long at all after meeting him that I was hopelessly in love. I attached every romantic notion to the entire relationship. He knew all the right things to say to a young girl in love for the first time. I stupidly believed everything he said of the life we'd have including wanting to marry me and take me back to the family farm and how much his "Mama was gonna love me." He took me to the Navy Exchange and purchased a half-karat pear-shaped diamond ring to make me his and his alone, he said.

"D" said he wanted to work on a family right away because of our 17-year age difference. He said he only had four months left on the base and two years left in the Navy so we needed to get the family established before he got discharged. I was thrilled. My head was in the clouds with this new direction my life was taking. I never felt coerced, sexually abused or traumatized. Although some of his sexual maneuvers were pretty intense and newly frightening to me, he said we'd work on them together until I did like it or we'd stop. I was beyond thrilled.

Assessing my life, I had it all—the sea breeze in my hair, a tropical island, a love affair for the ages and now baby on the way. The blood test confirmed what a night of lovemaking under the stars, on the beach with the waves lapping up over us only hinted at. "D" had wanted to get the family started and we now had that piece of our plan in place. The baby would be due in November, just shortly after "D" had rotated out of Cuba.

My imagination placed me in West Virginia at Christmas time with our new baby, on my family farm with my new husband. His mama was gonna love me, just as he said. And my mom was thrilled I was coming home to buy my wedding dress and "D's" ring. Together she and I did exactly that. It was a mother-daughter moment to cherish. He robbed us both of that memory too because of what a sham it revealed itself to be. Bastard.

I could barely contain myself when I went back to Cuba and went to see him. It was a quiet, private moment when I told him about the baby and showed him his wedding ring. His silence wasn't the tender response I expected. It was matter-of-fact, as though I said what I'd had for lunch that day. I was bewildered, but was sure it was the beginning of our new life together—admittedly less sure, but still believing.

This is where the most horrific experience of my life began. I say that now at 63 years old and looking back. The horror of it at 21 years old was almost more than I could handle—but I did handle it as best I could; not realizing it would impact the rest of my life so deeply.

When I became pregnant, the betrayal became all the more devastating.

Upon learning of my pregnancy, only then did his fellow MAA's tell me how much they'd enjoyed watching that all happen for me. I was so stupid. I took their meaning to be how they watched us fall in love—a bond of commitment form and the blessing of a marriage and the child to come—that they had enjoyed all that happening. I was so confused. It wasn't at all what they meant.

As "D's" fellow sailors/co-workers explained their meaning, I became horrified to learn the lovemaking of "D" and I had been great entertainment for all of them. They literally had been watching it all over the many previous weeks. "D" and I had used the police barracks as our love nest. It was safe where no one would find us or report us, I was told. I thought we were alone but we had been well observed. I'd been a sex toy for the observation of the five or six others who'd been on duty when I was in the dorm area with "D". What I thought was a secretive affair to protect my honor was sheer betrayal. The engagement ring gave it legitimacy and led me into a pattern of behavior in a secluded location with the man I loved.

So much more now made sense as the extent of the betrayal exposed itself: how others knew what was said in private, intimate moments; how others knew my sexual preferences and skills; how others knew my proficiencies and new experiences, reluctant actions and willing passions.

These were all being commonly discussed, enjoyed, observed and were now just disgusting points of verbal assaults by those who'd come to know me through watching my most private moments.

From late January 1974 to well into July 1974, I willingly visited "D" at the police station on leeward side. He would always make sure he or someone in his watch group drove me to the ferry landing for the last crossing of the night so I would be safe.

It was on one of those transports that a young sailor, as new to the Navy as was I, asked me if he could tell me something. He said I'd have to promise not to let on how I'd come to know. It was only when I did promise that this young man spoke in a soft, almost frightened voice. He said something to the effect of "You are going to be sad. "D" is married. His wife and son just shipped back to West Virginia less than six months ago," and then said, "I thought you didn't know but should."

I looked at his sweet face. I thought he was going to cry. I wanted to but no tears would come. But he was right. I was sad. I felt numb. I still hear his voice "I thought you didn't know, but you should." Now, when I do cry about it, I cry for the broken heart of an innocent girl.

It had all been nothing more than an ugly sex game for their gratification and amusement. I assured the young sailor I wouldn't let on what I now knew. He had the saddest eyes when he told me. He so wanted me to believe him when he promised he had 'never watched'. My heart sank. I felt like I'd been kicked in the gut. Cruelty. Betrayal. "D" had been just the next up-at-bat in their perfected game. It took me a lot of years to come to that conclusion. I was nothing to "D". I was nothing. I felt my innocence slip away like my satin hair ribbon coming undone and falling into the sandy dirt.

I decided to go see my "big brothers" of the Aviation Ordinance Division to find out what to do about the mess I was in. My blood-related brother was stationed in Cuba with me now. I feared telling him when it was a *problem*. I knew to come to him when I had a possible solution. I knew he'd love me unconditionally as he

17

always has but I didn't want him to react in a way that would damage or even destroy his career. I'd done enough damage to my own. I felt I'd been the prize in a very cruel and demeaning game of sexually intense moments. I was devastated, heartbroken, horrified and betrayed. I, somehow in all that, refused to be defeated.

The AO Division told me to get to medical to make them aware of my situation. I was given a full work-up, blood work, etc. I was told later I'd been given an X-ray with the faulty machine. I don't recall any X-ray but the Navy Corpsman, [a nice Italian boy from] Brooklyn New York insisted I had and to remember I did if ever asked. I found out later why it was important. It isn't in my medical records but I was to say I had one if asked. By now, I was 21 years old but still not smart enough to question or dispute anyone in authority over me.

The big brothers of the AO Division made a visit to the MAA station on leeward side. They called it "damage control/recon." Almost immediately, the verbalization and harassment ceased. I don't know who was there or exactly what was said. I was assured "all recordings" were destroyed. I was told no proof and no more replayed viewings of any kind remained of this horrible collaboration they had committed against me.

Whatever actions were taken on my behalf left me feeling my virtue had found a group of champions of my honor. The joy would be short-lived. My champions thought it best for all involved to sever any connection to me. Another loss. Only one sailor, AO1 "Smitty" from New England remained a dear and loyal friend. ("Smitty" even visited my family and me more than 10 years later as he passed through Chicago. He still kept my secret even then. I hadn't told my husband or anyone).

I think the reason we remained friends was because, at the end of all of the mess I had made of my time in Cuba, "Smitty" was the most honest with me as to how I got duped. He told me that LIFERS (career Navy sailors) while on isolated duty found it economically more effective to buy an engagement ring for their selected female sexual (target-victim) partner to guarantee a "steady piece of ass" than to have their wallets emptied by a lot of dates and never get laid for the money spent. It was brutally honest. It was said in front of half a dozen other AOs. They audibly gasped at "Smitty's" candor, thinking I'd be furious for him saying such a thing, or was it because he just gave up a major brotherhood secret.

It was demeaning and humiliating. I wasn't furious or outraged. I was numb. I had detached from my emotions. I felt like a dejected puppy kicked to the curb. I finally had an explanation as to why this was done to me. It didn't make it hurt any less but now I could see what an easy mark I was.

It was done for sport. It was done to pass the idle time. It was just "D's" turn to reap the benefits. But all the rest of them knew—and watched—and never stopped it. But for the gentle soul of a kind young boy finding the courage to tell me, I don't know how it all would have been resolved.

Now what was to be done with me was the bigger question. What was to become of the little person inside me? I made every effort to do nothing any differently. I appeared to maintain the engagement although I never seemed to have time to visit "D" on the leeward side again. I didn't let on knowing of "D's" wife and son. I prayed for an answer to be made known to me. I'd lost all confidence in my judgment. My prayers were endless. My sadness was not.

At my next medical appointment, I was given some very hard choices. I was asked if I'd had any X-ray upon arriving at GITMO or since being there. I remembered the [nice Italian] Corpsman telling me what to say if ever asked.

The X-ray machine at GITMO had been malfunctioning for an uncertain amount of time. There was concern that any pregnant female would almost certainly have exposure and increased probability of a malformed or significantly developmentally deficient child at birth. I had been convinced I was in this high risk exposure group.

Years later, I saw my medical report where the pregnancy was noted as "LOW RISK" but I had been told otherwise. So, in addition to the hateful manner in which the child was conceived, I was to have a child compromised due to faulty X-ray equipment. Was this God's punishment? Was HE even with me in this anymore? The X-ray of me had never happened. It was just my quick ticket out of Cuba for a procedure for something that was not my fault. Someone was trying to give me a good cover story so I could get an abortion without the guilt. It was decided for me to save me the guilt if I chose an abortion to save my career.

I was told I had the option of a medical discharge basically in disgrace and pregnant. I was still functioning under the false notion I was carrying a deformed child. I didn't see discharge as a viable option. How would I ever care for a special needs child? My other option was to go to Portsmouth Naval Hospital for an abortion. This was 1974. Abortion seemed like a vile proposition at best. The Corpsman I mentioned, [the nice Italian boy from] Brooklyn, cautioned me to just go have the abortion or I'd be drummed out of the Navy as just another whore sailor. He said I would get over the loss of "the kid" but I would never survive what would happen to me if I didn't go through with it.

If I wanted to continue in the Navy, then Portsmouth was the only option. It had always been my dream to be a mother but that perished with my innocence. I was not going to lose my dream of serving in the Navy too. The child I carried

19

had been conceived in a deceitful, adulterous adventure game by senior sailors at the expense of my innocence. Now the fates were going to take away the little life with no other viable option. What choice did I have really? As my Corpsman said: "go along to get along" and put this behind me. He also called it "Damage Control" as the AOs had.

I agreed to go to Portsmouth to terminate the pregnancy. It had been decided as what was best. I shut down all emotion. My faith was dead. I was numb. I asked "D" to meet me at the mess hall on Windward side for breakfast the next morning. It was the morning of **21 Jul 74.**

My brother was aware of the meeting. As he promised, others who were supportive of my plight, were there in the chow hall for my safety. I have no doubt many of them expected to witness a full-blown soap opera drama erupt. I was known to have a strong will and a reputation as a spitfire. I had no idea of what was to come.

I was disproportionately calm as I sat across the table from "D". I remember thinking what a low-life piece of garbage he was to have done such a thing to a little girl who loved him and trusted him so. I was repulsed at any thought of our intimacy. The room was a surreal sea of faces.

"D" was cheery and charming when he asked 'what was my plan-of-the-day?' I said, "Oh didn't I tell you? I'm transferring out today." I remember standing up and leaning toward him with my hands resting on the table. I wasn't screaming the words aloud but in my head it sounded like a PA system.

Screaming wasn't necessary. The mess hall got very quiet when I stood up. I was grinding my teeth and chewing each word as I said to him, "I know about your wife. Would you like me to stop by and show her my engagement ring and baby belly as I pass through Norfolk?" I went on to say I knew about the special views and shows he and I had put on for his division. I said that I knew it had all been a big sex game for him and his buddies. I asked how many other WAVES fell for this. I was told I was the only "stupid little girl" but that I'd been more than enough for all of them. I didn't believe then, nor do I now that I was the first or would be the last.

He had quite often called me a "stupid little girl" during the grooming romance but it was, I thought, directed toward my inexperience . . . no he meant just what he said now—*stupid little girl*.

I looked at the other sailors around the chow hall and made some veiled warning to the WAVES not to believe the liars and pigs. "D" all but laughed aloud at me when I spoke of them being the COPS and weren't they held to a higher standard, and weren't they supposed to protect, not break the law. He said something about 'nobody got hurt' and 'you seemed to enjoy it plenty enough.' The last words I heard from him were "Grow up, Stupid." I don't remember leaving the chow hall or even getting on the plane or arriving at Norfolk.

It wasn't the end of it. The horrors of Portsmouth Naval Station Hospital awaited me.

Incident #2

22 Jul 74 to 24 Jul 74 - NMC Portsmouth
24 Jul 74 to 20 Aug 74 -Naval Station Norfolk

So much of what happened after I left Cuba and before I got to NAS JAX, are in snapshot remembrances. Envision a sepia tone photo in your grandmother's album. Even as I read them in the documents I secured, I can marginally remember some of them and I don't recall others at all. I understand now how this is all part of the MST healing.

I think the trauma in the barracks added another layer of abuse to the medical crisis and trauma of what I was subjected to upon being readmitted to NMC Portsmouth. My first, brief stay at NMC Portsmouth was a whirlwind of unexplained moments. The process never slowed enough for me to get a grasp on what was actually happening. No information was shared with me as to my fate. I was kept off balance for those two days. By the time I got to the barracks, it was as if I had been primed by the hospital for the horrors ahead.

My biggest concern is what else happened at the barracks in my "lost time." Was it something so far beyond my coping mechanisms I had to block it off completely? What I do remember is horrible and I fear that much worse happened that I can't remember. I fear it's going to pop up to the forefront at any moment. Maybe nothing happened beyond what I recall. It is not knowing for sure if I have it inside me or I did survive everything and there is nothing else.

To this day, I still have an exaggerated startle response, moments of disassociation from what's happening around me, an unrealistic fear in crowds, and deeply rooted mistrust of people. This will get better with time. So I'm told. No signs of that yet. It's like a disjointed nightmare. I can't fully remember it, but what pieces of it I do remember still aren't sequencing any more clearly than when I slept. In the nightmare, faces and characters morph in appearance and intention with the threat level being the only constant. I'm in constant peril requiring constant hypervigilance. It will get better.

I left Cuba on **21 Jul 74** and checked into Naval Medical Center Portsmouth, Virginia on **22 Jul 74**. A whole new level of sexual trauma would damage me emotionally in the weeks ahead as I was housed in the [Norfolk women's] barracks. I was sent to Portsmouth for an abortion. I'd left Cuba with many other pregnant females on a medevac flight to receive abortions at Portsmouth. I was only kept two days at the hospital before being sent to the women's transient barracks at Naval Station Norfolk. My order said to hold me there for four weeks and return me to Portsmouth for the procedure when in my second trimester. *Why? Can you even have an abortion in the second trimester?* The entire ugly experience could have been handled immediately upon my arrival at NMC Portsmouth and I could get back on track with my Navy career. Why was my path detoured without my input or permission? Decisions were made, but it wasn't explained to me until I returned to Portsmouth. It was all very confusing and no one felt I was owed any explanation.

All these years I have kept my transfer orders and doctors notes and reports as proof of why my medical procedure was held over. I've also retained the history of assignment log sheets showing the inaccuracies of the actual locations and timeline of where I was assigned as compared to the entries. It has taken me since July 2014 to secure the medical and military records of this timeframe. It took multiple phone calls, emails, faxes and mailings, but no one would return any of the information I sought. I had all but given up as of January 15, 2015.

On March 26, 2015 all the records I had been trying to get for the past eight months showed up at my home; helping me reconstruct what happened. It's important to me that you, as my reader, know I am fully aware of the magnitude of the claims I make here. It is only because I was able to secure my records and reconstruct the events. While this puts the events in context, it still falls short of explaining why this was allowed or considered acceptable or ethical.

This timeframe and this incident pertains to the psychological, physical, emotional, and verbal abuse levied upon me while attached to the medical holding company awaiting the therapeutic abortion.

I was in NMC Portsmouth only two days. **22 Jul 74** to **24 Jul 74** before I was sent to the Naval Station Norfolk and put into the medical holding company. The barracks was eerily empty except for a few other in-transit WAVES. Some were awaiting reassignment, as I would be on **26 Aug 74**, some awaiting their transfer or discharge, while others remained in medical holding as was I.

I was purposefully assigned to barracks cleanup. I was ordered to use the strongest of cleaning solvents, bleaches, ammonia and the caustic orange floor scrubbing product without protection gear so the fumes might trigger a spontaneous abortion—their term, not mine—a miscarriage. The Corpsman [on duty that day] told me that "if your body throws it out naturally it won't be as painful as how we take it from you." Lord help me. I couldn't believe I was to intentionally poison myself and the baby I carried.

I was given restricted interaction with other females housed in the barracks due to my "disgraceful circumstances." I was billeted (assigned living and sleeping quarters) to a nearly deserted wing of the first floor. I had no one anywhere near me or my cubicle. The open bay dorm slept 80-120, but most of the cubicles weren't even set up for occupancy. I could hear someone at the other end but never saw them. I called out one night in the dark and the return response was "Quiet Whore!" I'd lie in my rack (bed) at night and cry, apologizing to the baby and saying goodbye. I spent every hour of the day and night alone with my thoughts. No point in speaking unless spoken to, as no one acknowledged the sound of my voice. I had to promise myself I would deal with it someday but for now, I just had to live through it.

I lied to my parents and family about why I was in Norfolk. Vietnam was winding down. So I told them special clearance would be needed. I said I couldn't have any visitors but I would come home before I was sent to my next duty station after this special assignment, if the Navy allowed it. I knew I could play off my somber and quiet demeanor (while healing from the procedure) as being appropriately concerned about the severity of the new training and the assignment I'd been given. They accepted the lie as the truth; said how proud they were of my commitment and service to my country, our country. Their words of support made my heart ever more hollow than before. I was now deceiving my support system. I had to protect them from the ugly truth and pain.

After a particularly bad bout of morning sickness, or toxic poisoning, I recall the MAA of the barracks, some harsh and hardened 1st Class Petty Officer female standing over me as I puked. She picked her moment for confronting me. She berated me, more gloating, "You just aren't going to let go of IT, are you?" With that, she ordered me to run the floor buffer and to hold it close to my 3 1/2-month baby belly to try and "shake it loose." I thought she was walking away when I turned my back but she swooped up behind me, grabbed the buffer handle and abruptly pulled it up and into my abdomen from behind me. I don't remember what happened next, or for weeks after. Much of my time in Norfolk/Portsmouth is in episodic moments of horror and pain, lots of new faces and awful people hurting me. I was isolated in every sense and safe nowhere.

The next recollection I have is of being on the 2nd floor lounge of the barracks on **9 Aug 74** as our Commander-in-Chief, President Richard M. Nixon, resigned on television. That time frames it for me. I stood there leaning on a mop handle and I was still pregnant.

Then a phone call came. A friendly voice felt foreign to my ears. It was [my nice Italian] Corpsman [calling] from Cuba, alerting me he'd been transferred. He would be passing through Norfolk. He hoped I could get him from the base airfield at NAS Cecil Field to the civilian airport so he could get up to Brooklyn for leave on his way to his next duty station. I was so hungry for a kind word and someone—anyone—who would be happy to see me. I, of course, said yes. I told him I'd arrange everything and asked if he would be in town long or just passing through? [He] said he'd set aside one night over to check in on me and offer his support in what he thought must be a "tough assignment for a kid." Okay. Maybe there were still a few good guys left. I found myself looking forward to seeing him.

An odd occurrence awaited me. When I went to pick up [my nice Italian Corpsman] at the air terminal, Naval Air Station Cecil Field, I was not prepared for what happened.

Following the odd occurrence (I don't know if it was a week or month) I was back in the Naval Medical Hospital in Portsmouth with some of the other women who had been on the medevac flight out of Cuba. I know now because I got my medical records and was able to reconstruct where I was and when things were happening to me and around me. The admission slip to the hospital, says it was **20 Aug 74**. I would be there [in NMC Portsmouth] for six days.

The [following is the story of the] odd occurrence [that] awaited me.

An Odd Occurrence
Leave Your Baggage at the Gate

I had been so quick to tell my nice Italian Corpsman I would happily drive him to the civilian airport that I neglected to mention I didn't have a vehicle.

As I drove to the military airfield in the car I had rented, I felt genuinely cheerful for the first time in months. I was cute as a button, pregnant and glowing when I arrived at the Navy air terminal to retrieve him. I even went so far as to put on my engagement ring—just to avoid questions (at least, that's what I told myself). I let everyone just assume I was married and my nice Italian Corpsman would be, unknowingly, the presumptive father. *Where was the harm in that? Let me have an appearance of normalcy. Nothing in my current daily life had any normalcy to it, so why the hell not?*

I joined all the other Navy families awaiting the return of their loved ones from isolated duty in Cuba. Flitting about and not getting too specific concerning my connection to the inbound flight or my maternity, I just enjoyed the moment. As I waited, I moved from one happy conversation to another.

The air terminal stunk from years of jet fumes and stale cigarettes. The sweat of sailors and soldiers hung in the air. My hormonal sense of smell had my nose wrinkling up and my stomach flipping erratically. Yet the room was buzzing with such happy chatter and anticipation that I couldn't help but feel part of it.

All too abruptly, the feeling of euphoria vanished. It was as though an enormous, ominous, dark cloud had blocked out the sun. Time then shifted into such surreal slow motion that it seemed almost deliberately orchestrated to allow me to reason out exactly what was taking place.

A little woman in her late 30s or early 40s, with short dark hair approached me. She had an engaging smile and was as excited as everyone else was. She seemed harmless enough at first. She struck up a conversation with me, just as I had done earlier with so many others. The tone was pleasant, the topics superficial. The pleasantries didn't last, however.

This frail, weary woman apparently felt she had found a sympathetic ear and began sharing her story of separation from her husband due to his isolated duty in Cuba. She spoke of how hard it was on her and their teenage boy with his dad (her husband) still in Cuba. *(Still?)* She explained the family had been together in Cuba with him but had to return stateside about eight months ago. She said it was okay at first but then he had stopped sending money home and she and her son were struggling to get by.

I expressed how hard I imagined it must have been for them. I sympathized while simultaneously beginning to realize who this woman was. She said it didn't take her long to find out via the Navy grapevine that her "pig of a husband" had gotten involved with some "WAVE slut" who was trying to break up their marriage. She went on in greater detail about the pregnancy leverage and the real fear she had of losing her husband. My ears were throbbing with a numbing heat. The air terminal took on a suffocating, illusionary pallor.

Oh Lord, help me. This was "D's" wife standing right before me. I knew it, but she had no idea I was the "WAVE slut" she maligned. Her words were now nothing more than a drone of venomous attacks. *Oh Lord, help me.* This needed time to sink in but time was a luxury I didn't have. I snapped out of the fog of her endless barrage of words when she said, "My husband, "D", is going to be on this plane and I can't wait to wring his neck."

I had a flashback to the last time I spoke to "D" in the mess hall in Cuba. How prophetic my threatening question seemed now—*'Would you like me to stop by and show my engagement ring and baby belly to your wife as I pass through Norfolk?'* The stars of the cosmos had aligned.

I recalled the three words of my father's admonishment throughout my childhood when I was about to make a big mistake, as I shouted them silently to myself - *DON'T DO IT!*

So many questions flooded my head. Is this why I was put in this place at this time? Is this why circumstances delayed the abortion in order to punish me with her words or present me with the gift of meeting "D's" wife? Is this why my

Italian Corpsman asked me to pick him up at the terminal? Did he know "D" would be on the flight? Why was this happening?

All those questions were going to have to wait because the arrival of the plane was announced. The crowd moved as one toward every open doorway of the hanger to greet the sailors as they exited the aircraft. The entire ritual took on a life of its own. I let "D's" wife take my hand as she guided me through the sea of families. What an odd caring moment it was. Would she have been so kind had she known who I was? Surely not.

As I stood there next to her, cold as stone on a 95-degree day, we waited in silence. What a gift I was about to receive! *Life's a bitch and her stripper name is Karma.* I say that now at 63 having known a lifetime of ironies, but as a frightened, very pregnant little girl at 21 I was just exactly that— frightened. Paralyzed by fear and anticipation.

There it was—the look on "D's" face was sheer terror. Every fear my heart had endured for my unknown future now showed itself all over *his* face. "D" first saw his wife. He smiled the charming smile he'd used on me. She smiled and waved back at him. Then "D" saw who stood next to her.

There it was—"D's" stark panic. She saw his face when he saw my face, and then she turned to look at me. She looked back at him. She looked back at me. She was heartbroken as all doubt sank like a 30-ton anchor to the bottom of the deep, blue sea. It didn't feel good for me to see her like that regardless of all the things she said in the hours prior. It *did* feel outrageously fulfilling to see the abject fear on "D's" face. (Oh, and he had a black eye from the send-off he'd been given by my friends in Cuba. I thoroughly enjoyed seeing that.)

I looked at her crestfallen face. She was devastated. *You poor thing,* I thought to myself. *You're married to this piece of crap.* There was nothing mean or vindictive I could say. I never even imagined a day when I might meet her, yet here it was. She said little, as she no doubt was reviewing everything she had said to me and about me in the two hours prior during which we had waited together in the air terminal.

As the silence between us seemed to stretch out forever, I took her hand, placed my engagement ring in it and closed her fingers around it. As I held her fist in my hands, I said, "That's right. I am 'her'. I know now that he used money he should have been sending home to you to buy this ring for me, and for that I am sorry. I'm so very sorry for all of this."

Just then, I realized my Italian Corpsman was standing there behind me. He heard it all. I'd never even seen him get off the plane. He wrapped his arm around my shoulder and commented that I'd had enough excitement for one day. The words went unsaid but his meaning was clear, and I was so very happy to have him take control of the situation as "D" approached.

My mind was reeling—frantic, manic and fraught with panic. *What the hell just happened?* My thoughts of what I should've said, could've said, would've said if I had known she was going to be there all amounted to nothing.

It was done. All things considered, it had gone remarkably well. No ugly scene. I walked away feeling less like a victim and more like I'd somehow been spared. Even in my situation, it was "D's" wife I felt warranted the pity.

My Italian Corpsman and I drove to his hotel laughing about the conversation we imagined was taking place in the not-so-happy couple's vehicle on *their* drive away from the terminal. As I dropped him at his hotel, he asked if I'd made plans for dinner. I admitted my social calendar was experiencing a bit of a dry spell, as I patted my belly. I commented I was always hungry these days.

I don't recall where my Italian Corpsman took me to eat but back at the hotel he wasn't shy about asking me to stay the night. Just for a moment, I did consider it. I even joked about his not having to worry about knocking me up as that already seemed to have been done.

Then, in the sweetest and almost clumsily of ways, he spoke from his heart. He said that he thought, maybe, I would like someone to hold me and tell me it was all going to be all right. He said I could cry if I needed to and he would hold me until I was done. He said he would rub my feet or brush my hair, or even wash my back if I wanted a bubble bath. What he did insist was that we could not and would not have sex. He spoke of a girl up in Brooklyn whom he loved. He said we could cuddle and he would hold me while I slept but he must remain faithful to her.

For a split second I thought, *Whoa, this guy has a line!* as I wondered if it usually worked for him. But the offer was too good to pass up. My heart wanted to know what trust and security felt like again even if for one night. I stayed the night. I skipped the bubble bath but I got in as much crying and cuddling as 12 hours could hold.

I heard about the young girl who was the love of my Italian Corpsman's life. I silently wished for a man who would one day love me so completely. I wondered if maybe in future years as they grew old together, he might share with her what a wonderful thing he had done for me.

I heard all about Brooklyn and his family. He proudly spoke of being the grandson of an old-world Italian lady who was famous for her pizza. I still smile fondly each time I see an iconic picture of an old-world Italian woman or bake a tasty pizza. In my heart, I thank her for the kindness instilled in him in his upbringing. He shared a night of the most sincere compassion I'd ever known in my life to that point. What a nice Italian boy. What a lucky girl awaited him in Brooklyn.

My visit with my favorite Corpsman gave me the respite to survive the remainder of what awaited me in the barracks back at Norfolk Naval Station. Sadly, it didn't sustain me when I was readmitted to Navy Medical Center, Portsmouth on **20 Aug 74.** Nothing could have prepared me for that.

Incident #3

20 Aug 74 to 26 Aug 74 - Naval Medical Hospital - Portsmouth, VA

As it was explained to me at Naval Hospital, Portsmouth, we had all been marking time so we'd be in our second trimester for a fetus gestation study to be done at this teaching hospital. It was just gossip from the other women who'd arrived from Cuba with me, so I found it hard to believe. It was actually some new dilation drug study of [a] seaweed-like compressed stick that would be inserted vaginally to cause the cervix to dilate causing labor to begin prematurely rather than putting us through the more invasive suction abortion. I had started to wonder, was I going to be a lab rat?

In my [later] search [at 62 years old] to complete my claim to the VA, no one at NHS Portsmouth could provide proof of the trial. I called and emailed multiple times. My first call was well received and encouraging. I was told they kept the medical trial documents on site for 40 years and I was getting in just under the wire. The research doctor who took my call said he knew of the study and knew just where the information could be found but he asked how I had heard of it. I admitted I was one of the subjects. No information was forthcoming. When I contacted him again at the email address he'd given me, no responses were sent. No calls were returned.

[At 21 years old] when I reported back to NHS Portsmouth from my barracks assignment, I was told I'd been chosen to take part in the study and was told I would willingly submit to the protocols. I remember it distinctly because it was the first time I'd ever heard the word "protocols" and I had to ask what it meant. I was ordered, not offered. I protested that perhaps there would be side effects or it may disable me from having children in the future. I stated I was not interested and did not want to take part in the study. I was then asked, "You are still in the Navy, are you not? And you do still take orders, don't you?" "Then it's decided." All choice removed, I complied. Oh my God! I *am* going to be their lab rat!

The RN noted in the chart on **20 Aug 74** at 3:11 [a.m.] that I asked for a Chaplain and "still appeared somewhat hostile." I feel I had good cause. I have kept the chart notes, along with the consent forms I was strong-armed into signing.

Now with the medical records in hand, I have the doctor's narrative summary of the procedure dated **20 Aug 74** for the procedure done **21 Aug 74**. [Date order not a typo, btw.]

31

I knew of the seaweed-like stick being inserted in me because I asked while it was happening and asked what they were doing. But there it was documented in the narrative along with the statement of prostaglandins being used.

Prostaglandins were only discovered in the early 1970s. I had been used as a guinea pig in the rapid evolution of their use and pivotal role they would play in obstetrics in the future. I have since accumulated medical articles stating it was an emerging field of study in the '70s regarding prostaglandins. It has become common now.

The hospital staff made their rounds twice daily. I was ordered to expose my vaginal area by grabbing the backs of my knees and spread-eagle so the 8-10 medical students and Navy officers could observe the insertion of the seaweed stick, now known to be the Luminaria tent. [Then began the] examination of my cervix by any of the amateurs who wanted to stick their fumbling hands up my vagina with less skill than a clumsy teenage boy at a drive-in movie. Three or four of the young Navy doctors in succession usually gave it an effort.

Each time I was ordered to present my vagina into position, I raised the sheet above my legs and pulled it up further to cover my face. I just let the tears roll down my cheeks. No point in crying out loud. No one cared. I remember the camera flash and the noise of the Polaroid camera film advancing during one of those episodes. I thought how relieved I was my face was covered. How sad I was to be reduced to a faceless vagina for the Navy's use as theirs.

I was so far removed from the "stupid little girl" who had conceived a baby in a love affair once thought to be the stuff of romantic storybooks. I found myself hoping for a side effect of toxic shock or death.

But labor came. The baby was born; horribly malformed—their words, not mine, but said so I could hear—from the cleaning solvents or maybe the other physical trauma. Only recently did I read the Dr.'s narrative. "Baby never drew a breath," the nurse told me. She said, "By God's grace." I never asked the gender. Thank God they never offered. It wasn't in the medical records for which I am so very grateful . . . by God's grace. Apparently God wasn't done with me yet. It seems the seaweed stick device they were testing in the trial caused the uterus/placenta or afterbirth to shred—as was warned in the medical articles written so many years later.

There were two nurses caring for me. Two sets of chart notes. I was put through a full labor and delivery. The nurses' notes do not agree with each other. One set says the placenta was expelled intact, the other says nothing of it. There would have been no need for a D&C if it had been intact. The pathologist's report refers to testing a *fragment* of the placenta. You don't get a fragment from an intact placenta. The conflicting notes scream inaccuracy and brings question as to the truthfulness of some of the entries and documentation.

The corpsmen were now going to give me a D&C. They almost looked excited by the prospect. I didn't know what a D&C was or what was involved or how serious it was. Nothing was explained to me. No anesthetics were given. The medical students gathered around, almost in an animated or enthusiastic atmosphere of what was to come.

Three corpsmen/interns took me to an examination room in a makeshift Operating Room. It had pull-around drapes and seemed lacking somehow in formal surgical surroundings and sanitary precautions. It felt wrong. I recall a certain dread of something awful about to happen, as if the past 24 hours hadn't been horrific enough.

[Still] no anesthetics were given. It was after hours, early evening. I remember staring at a wall clock. I noticed how largely out of proportion it seemed to the room. I don't remember what time it said but I kept thinking *Time will pass, no one will stop the clock, it won't last forever* There was a blur of surgical lights blinding me so I closed my eyes. Suddenly someone, no it had to be two people, simultaneously strapped my ankles into the stirrups and then my arms lashed into leather. I remember the feel of the sheets as I gathered them into my fists and clinched them tightly.

My screams of pain were ignored. I remember the sound of my uterus being scraped out. It made me think of the noise of cleaning the guts out of a pumpkin with a spoon scraping the side walls before carving a Jack-O-Lantern—I still can't tolerate the sound, and I flash back. Each drag of the surgical instrument scraping along the wall of my now empty womb emitted a moaning from me. One of the corpsmen said that maybe I needed some painkillers. One of the others said, very coldly, "Maybe this will teach you - remember how this feels the next time you wanna open your legs." With that, he gave me a solid jab internally to emphasize his point.

The other two males in the room chuckled. I don't recall any females in the room or around me at all that night; not even a nurse. Doubtful they'd have been sympathetic to my plight. But it wouldn't have mattered anyway. No one cared.

No one stopped the clock. The D&C finally ended. I awoke back in the ward in the bed where the delivery occurred. With a tear-stained wet pillow, it only took me a minute to realize it had been me crying in my dream and my crying caused me to wake up. More lost time.

I know I had seen the Chaplain often after my first request. It may have been something I'd said because I do remember screaming and crying a lot after the procedure. I remember the phrase, "I just need to go home!" and I know I was saying it often and while crying in panic.

"I just need to go home." I don't know who I was saying it to or in what context, during the timeframe after the D&C and before they finally did let me go home. I remember the feel of the hospital linens; I remember the bedside visits from the Chaplain. I know I saw him after I got out of the hospital and was sent back to the barracks in Norfolk to await orders. I know in my heart it was the Chaplain who took pity and ordered I be sent home on leave.

I was given leave and I remember I did go home for a visit. I know I got to NAS Jacksonville on **14 Sep 74.** I'd left Cuba on **21 Jul 74**. I hadn't seen the records until April 2015 so I was now able to pin down the dates. So now I knew the date of the procedure was **21 Aug 74.**

I went home. I don't know what comfort I expected because I had no intention of sharing the truth of the last six weeks. I didn't tell anyone any of it. Maybe just the sameness of a small town upbringing was all I needed. There were the same people, the same routines, smells, noises of a simple life and childhood I wanted to recapture. I visited the city park and the trails I walked in my youth. I felt very old and tired for my 21 years. The surroundings did restore my sense of self. It rejuvenated my decision to be Navy— not just be in it, but *be* NAVY.

Praise for my service to country came from all directions as I was seen around town. It made my heart swell and my wounds heal enough to take a deep breath, go back to the military life I'd chosen; to go be the person everyone believed me to be. I planned to be career Navy.

I took my newfound resolve—not even "new"—"restored" more accurately described it, and I was off to NAS JAX for new beginnings. I arrived at NAS Jacksonville Florida **14 Sep 74.**

Incident #4

Late Spring/Early Summer 1975 - NAS Jacksonville, FL - NISO Investigator

I arrived at NAS JAX on **14 Sep 74**. Within one year and two days, I was promoted to E-4.

After Cuba and after Portsmouth, because I'd '*gone along to get along*' like my nice Italian Corpsman had advised was best, I did get to pick my orders. I just wanted to feel safe again. My brother, Neil[1], was still in Cuba. He'd get no-cost orders to NAS JAX when his tour ended. We would have brother/sister duty again. I could feel safe again.

I thought it would be a fresh start, with the sadness and deceit of Cuba [along] with all the mess that followed at Portsmouth behind me. But it wasn't to be. Wishing didn't make it so. Hope carried me forward.

It hadn't been all bad in Cuba. It was an amazing time there. Professionally, it was the most meaningful chapters in my five years of service. I learned so much and I contributed historically, as one of the first fifty (50) female Operations Specialists when the rate was converted from Radarman. I felt I owed it to the women of the Navy not to screw up.

Personally, it was the most tragic because a child was sacrificed. The loss of my innocence was just collateral damage, a casualty of the culture. I'd left there [Cuba] trusting no one and having nothing to return to in civilian life if I left the Navy. I accepted the loss of the child through the way I was coerced and manipulated; and I vowed I had indeed learned my lesson. My heart was stone cold and I was as alone as I could ever imagine. It was the way I wanted it. I was happy with not feeling, not wanting to feel and wanting no one to feel anything for me.

All this being acknowledged, I was hopeful that NAS Jacksonville was my fresh beginning. When I got to NAS JAX, I dismissed the looks I got to being just the new WAVE on base. It was a pretty common occurrence. A new face always raised interested curiosity. I ignored it.

It didn't take me long to realize my "unpleasantness" in Cuba had been told and retold to the sailors at NAS JAX. I'd get confirmation of it much later in my tour, but for now it [felt like] more than [just] a guilty mind feeling suspicious. No privacy protection of HIPAA back in 1974.

35

In my first performance appraisal covering **14 Sep 74** to **28 Feb 75,** I was praised for my positive contribution despite my "feelings and personal problems." I had told no one of any personal problems. I was secretive even by my standards. But they already knew.

There was also an entry in my medical record in March 1974 referencing my "history in GITMO" which resulted in me being re-evaluated for risk to have my Secret Security Clearance revoked. It was upheld and I retained my clearance with no lapse. The collateral damage had no impact on my ability to perform my job.

I resolved to serve without distraction. I focused on my duty assignment. I lived in the barracks until my brother, Neil, got to NAS JAX. I didn't mix in or date. NAS JAX had brought a fresh opportunity to focus on my career and my future. I vowed to keep myself to myself. *So what* if they knew or thought they knew? There was no confidentiality back then. Let their small minds distract them. It wasn't going to distract me from focusing forward.

I fell back on old friendships with trusted classmates from "A" School in Great Lakes back in the fall [season] of 1973. I reconnected with ENG 1st Class "S.D."—an old boyfriend who I'd met while he was attending a "C" school also in the fall of 1973. "S.D." was stationed at Naval Station Charleston, a safe distance away; not under foot every day, not a distraction. Life seemed stable again both personally and professionally.

I was befriended at NAS JAX by Commander Alvin Marsh[2] who was the Executive Officer of what would be my brother's ATC Division at the air terminal at NAS JAX. I felt that when Neil transferred up from Cuba all the pieces of the puzzle would fit back in place again. Neil and I were lucky enough to find a house to share on Lake Shore Boulevard, off Blanding in Jacksonville on the St John's River about 25 minutes from the base.

Commander Marsh became my 'Sea Daddy'—a mentor and to this day someone I still very much admire. We stay in touch. Al's presence in my life at NAS JAX kept others with bad intent away from me. It [my presence in his life] also kept [away] the other young WAVES who viewed him as a hot ticket to advance their careers. They viewed me to be territorial in my role as his protector. He needed protecting. He was vulnerable, but he was my protector as well. It was a mutually beneficial relationship. Together we laughed at those with predatory intention. We let them think what they would of our closeness, while we knew the truth. Worse things had been said about me and I'd survived. Al Marsh is a man of honor and integrity. He restored my faith in the authenticity of our leaders – the Brass of the Navy. CDR Marsh actually attended my wedding in August of 1978, flying my brother up from NAS JAX to NAS Glenview so they both could attend the ceremony and reception. In short, I trusted CDR Marsh, his judgment, his advice and guidance. I respect him still.

I refocused my attention on my skills as an Operations Specialist and my performance evaluations reflected positively upon my statistical abilities, my attention to detail and my dedication to duty.

My trips up to Charleston Naval Base to see 1st Class Petty Officer "S.D." became more frequent but my determination to have a solid military career remained in the forefront of my priorities. I resolved not to allow my personal life to be under foot in my daily routine. I vowed to maintain a strong separation between duty and my personal life. Separation by miles or emotional distance was my control mechanism. It was effective and efficient.

This was to be my final visit to Charleston to see 1st Class Petty Officer "S.D."—he was stationed on the USS Inchon—LPH 12 and was now living off-base with three sinister civilians in a house in Folly's Beach. We had gone out to dinner in the black Lincoln Continental of one of the new roommates. These guys wanted to impress me by taking me to a seafood steakhouse, "The Atlantic." It was a high dollar, old southern money, rustic ranch style building up on stilts, moss dripping from cypress trees and only top shelf liquor. No way was I ever otherwise going to afford being seated at a linen covered table inside The Atlantic; not on Navy pay. As we exited the car and were nearly to the entrance, the driver said, "Back to the car, all of you. Now!" I'm thinking what the hell is going on? I did as I was told. As we all stood at the trunk of the massive barge of a car, the driver started to chuckle. As he popped open the trunk, he commented they were all probably carrying a bit too much weight to be going to dinner. Now I'm thinking what the hell, now we aren't going to dinner? I watched while all the men, except "S.D." removed multiple guns from various places on their persons.

I looked into the trunk. I saw their guns, a cloth bag with lots of loose money, lots of heavy linked chain and tarps. What the hell indeed! I said nothing. I didn't want to end up in the trunk. I was out of my league. I saw their guns, their cars, the amount of money being thrown around and exchanged for drugs. I saw the hashish and marijuana at the Folly Beach cabin. As frightened as I was, I was more concerned for the safety of our sailors at Naval Station Charleston and the security of the base and ships. I was angry at myself for falling into such company but I was frightened to my core.

I found myself compelled to report "S.D." to NISO (Naval Investigative Services Office). I wanted to speak to CDR Marsh almost immediately, because of what I was seeing up in Charleston. Until I could leave to return to NAS JAX, I kept my eyes open and my mouth shut. I was beyond frightened.

What I observed was an elaborate drug operation supplying NS (Naval Station) Charleston. In truth, I didn't know the full extent of the misdoings. I saw a lot of pieces and clues but I didn't have the full picture. I knew enough not to ask questions. I already knew enough to know it was wrong on a level far beyond my pay grade or understanding. Once I knew of the criminal acts, how would I distance myself? I now knew something I didn't want to know.

I wanted to speak to CDR Marsh. He was in my thoughts, knowing his level of integrity kept me calm, while I planned my exit. He was a principled leader. I knew if I could get to him then he'd advise me wisely. Chaos raged in my head. Staying calm was imperative.

I couldn't get out of there fast enough. But I didn't want to look panicked. I cut my trip short and returned to NAS Jacksonville. It was a long trip back. I came to some very hard drawn conclusions. Upon returning to work Monday morning, I sought out CDR Marsh. He agreed with the conclusions I'd come to on my own during my drive back. I would need to report it to NISO immediately and distance myself from "S.D.", from Charleston, from all of it.

Within days of returning to NAS JAX I sought out NISO. This was approximately late spring/early summer of 1975. I was not comfortable ratting out someone for whom I had strong emotional feelings. It weighed on my mind how recent history demonstrated my poor judgment when tied to emotional entanglements. In short, I didn't trust my judgment. I had no doubt there was cause to be fearful of the civilian associates of Petty Officer "S.D.". I could not be afraid of losing his friendship. I had to protect my career. I had to tell NISO, step back and stay clear of it.

The house at Folly's Beach was on a peninsula-like piece of property. It was booby trapped and guarded on three sides by large attack dogs. The waterside approach was always guarded by the man watching for deliveries to come by boat. The roof of the cabin was used for more than sunbathing as I was told when yelled at to "get off the roof or else." Walkies were used to communicate. I only had the one contact with a guard. There were three or four guards who never spoke. It seemed like they never slept. The guards didn't sleep in the cabin with us although there were five bedrooms and it was a two-story cinder-block structure—more than a cabin. They were always on the property and always watching.

All this being known to me, I thought my best protection was to report it to NISO. I told what I knew in an interview to two investigators. I told them I didn't want to be seen going in and out of the offices of NISO on base. I was the one to initiate off-site contact. I was very sure word would get back to NS Charleston. I was suspicious of everyone and trustful of very few. I was assured of my safety at every step of the process.

As the investigation progressed over the next few weeks, I was told by one of the two investigating agents that going forward he was to be my direct contact. I was not to go to the on-base offices of NISO and to call there only in an absolute emergency. This investigator would contact me as discreetly as possible. I was to tell no one else. We would meet off base as if by chance. He did show up when I least expected and without warning. He said it was all for my safety. I'd be a CI (Confidential Informer), never have to testify and never be "found out" as the source of the information used to take down the drug ring. I was told my info was very accurate and I'd saved lives by coming to NISO. I felt at ease with my decision. I couldn't wait to tell CDR Marsh but then I remembered I was to tell no one. Oh, how I would come to regret not telling him. It might have saved me.

On the very next weekend I went to an off-base party in Jacksonville with a group of WAVES. I thought I saw one of the creepy guys who frequented the house at Folly's Beach in Charleston. My instincts said this was not a party I should be at if this type civilian was there. I also thought he may recognize me or be looking for me. I had my own car so I feigned a headache and left before I was seen. I called my NISO agent Monday morning. He said I was to tell no one else. I said I hadn't. He snarled, "Don't!" He said he would find me later.

Very soon after that, he contacted me again. He said he'd developed enough of a lead from my tip to have me attend a party where I may recognize some of the crowd from the visits I'd made to Charleston. I was asked if I would be brave enough to follow through in the accusations/information I'd given NISO. He assured me I'd be safe because he'd have other undercover drug agents there. Because it had crossed state lines, federal agencies, and military bases, I'd be taken care of and I'd be safe.

I was just 22 years old. I was so naïve. Now at 63 years old, after a 20-year career in law enforcement, I can look back on who I was then and realize without a doubt, I was being groomed. I was being groomed by a skilled predator for what was going to happen at the *party* I was to attend. Every maneuver, every scenario of this agent fed my need for safety and worthiness and my desire to contribute to the greater good and serve my country with pride and honor. He groomed me with the skills of a master. He said every word I needed to hear to secure my trust in him. I knew what was happening in Charleston was above my pay grade but this agent was far above my league.

I arrived at the address I was given by the NISO Investigator. As he instructed, I came alone, dressed to party and told no one where I was going. Looking back, that was not too smart of me. I was playing right into his hands.

I think it was a Friday night but I don't recall working that day so it may have been a Saturday. I guess it doesn't matter. It is such a small detail. I shouldn't give it more weight than it deserves. I do remember having a full day to recover before going on duty. I just don't fully recall what day it was. It haunts me. I need to let it go.

It was a really nice complex, very upscale and exclusive looking. I remember being impressed and excited as I walked up to the building with the wide sidewalks and lush palms, landscaping and flowers. It was all well-manicured and deliberate. I was pretty full of myself in these new surroundings. I felt I was elevating my life, my standing.

I heard the loud music as I approached the apartment door on the 2nd or 3rd floor I mustered my courage and knocked. Life as I knew it was about to change completely. As the door opened, I only noticed a long darkened hallway behind the guy opening the door. At first, I was surprised and then relieved to see my investigator answer the door. He was dressed very much in civilian casual, Florida mid-'70s scruffy style. I didn't acknowledge knowing him in case those inside would hear me. I said what I was told to tell the guy who opens the door. "Hi! I'm here to party!" I followed him down the hallway to a well-furnished luxury apartment.

I said, "I'm a little embarrassed for being the first one to arrive. When are the others coming?" He said, "You are the party tonight." Panic stricken, heart racing and thinking *Run! Run! Run!* But I said, "This is a bad idea. Maybe I should go. Wouldn't we compromise the investigation by getting involved?" Every bit of information I'd given him would be compromised.

I said, "I'm going to leave." He told me, "Just have a drink, hear what I have to say. If you still want to leave, then we will call it a night." I made the wrong choice. I should have followed my instincts to leave upon arriving. I chose to stay for the drink out of fear of what would happen if I didn't. I played right into his manipulation. I'd hear him out and then I could leave. LIAR!

It soon became clear to me my host had started drinking or had ingested something prior to my arrival. He was sexually and verbally aggressive almost immediately. I had not seen any hint of this side of him prior to that night. I was told the evening would continue in this vein if I did not "show a little more cooperation with the investigation." Was this some weird cop game?

He asked questions about Charleston; about the people; about the drugs in the house at Folly's Beach. All information we had covered before completely in the past weeks. He was acting like an investigator but was so impaired it was menacing and perverted.

I was starting to look around for the safest way to leave the apartment. I looked for the bathroom—just anywhere or any way out of there. He commented on me looking skittish as he crossed the living room and sat uncomfortably close to me. He started playing with my hair and telling me how beautiful I was; how innocent. I thought of Cuba for a flash—nope, no longer innocent. I'd only had the one drink but the whole night was feeling out of control or headed that way. I went into full survival thinking mode. Flee or fight?

I jumped up. It seemed to startle us both. I said, "Hey. A lady needs to use the bathroom. You just need to relax." I actually was going to bolt for the door. I must have telegraphed it. I chickened out when I saw how quickly he responded. He redirected me toward the bathroom. I started crying, not openly but in fear, just hoping to get out of there unhurt. I was trapped. I knew it. I just didn't know what was to happen next.

My thoughts were racing and my heart was pounding. Just as I headed for the bathroom and I could see into it on my right, I felt his hands land heavy on my shoulders as he came up behind me. He changed my direction by twisting me to the left. He said, 'We are going in here first . . ."

Before I could resist physically or even verbally, he shoved me into a bedroom and said in a menacing slur, "We can and will start the party now." He was muscular, physically fit and very much stronger than I. I'd never given thought or notice to that before. This man who I once thought so highly of was pure evil.

It was now more than a passing thought to me. To get out of this unhurt was no longer the driving thought for me—just getting out of this *alive* was. My three older brothers always told me, as crass as it sounds, if I got in a crisis such as this - *Don't get yourself hurt or worse over a piece of ass. It isn't worth it. Just survive it and we [can] even the score later.* At that moment, I was ready to settle for that. It was a stupid thing to remember at just that moment but it probably saved my life. My brothers had said it so often throughout my adolescence it popped into my head as loudly as if Jim, my deceased brother, was right there saying it to me at that very second. I believe his spirit was. Think what you will.

I told the investigator we could stop where this was going. No one would know it had gone too far. Just as he had told me; I hadn't told anyone and I wouldn't. No one would know I was there. He came right back with, "Exactly." He said no one would know what was about to happen next. If they should find out then he would deny everything. I would not be believed once they were told I'd followed him home to persuade him not to turn me in for my part in the NS Charleston drug sales. Everything in the investigation would be slanted to include me as a principle participant. All those trips I'd made back and forth to Charleston and the men I'd seen at the off-base party would all identify me as the connecting piece and transport/supplier of the drug sales expanded down to Jacksonville. By showing up at his apartment to offer him sexual persuasion to make me a CI he resisted all temptation and would charge me with attempting to bribe an agent and interfering with a NISO investigation. He was so smug when he asked, "Who do you think they'll believe?"

I tried to head for the door. He blocked my path. He reached back and locked the door. He said, "Aren't ya glad now that you stayed? I told you you'd want to hear me out. You'd be foolish to leave; I will ruin you. No one will be looking for you. No one will find you. No one will miss you: *poor girl killed by drug dealers, she had so much potential.*" Each word sealed my fate. I felt broken.

He taunted me when he said, "Remember you said you had nothing to return to in civilian life? I will be sure you have less than nothing. If you still want to leave, there's the door."

I sat on the edge of the bed considering my choices versus his size, his altered state of alcohol, drugs, and predatory aggressive anger. I heard my brother's words—'*it's just a piece of ass, not worth dying over'*—and then I thought about CDR Marsh. If I could get through this, then he'd help me. I thought of my brother, Neil, who would soon be stationed with me again. He and I would come back after this guy later. My mind was racing. My heart was racing. I couldn't let it show.

The quieter I became, I might have looked like I was more willing, more submissive. I don't know what he was thinking. I wasn't thinking clearly. *Had he put something in my drink?* The investigator said I shouldn't take too long to consider his offer. I stood to say, "What offer? What choice?" I was angry. I stood too abruptly. He jumped off the bed and said, "Times up!" He threw me down on the bed and pinned me by my wrists. I yipped in pain. He said that he didn't have to hurt me unless I wanted it that way tonight. I said, "No don't. I don't want it any way from you, pain or not. Stop now." Wrong answer.

I was told I was "gonna get it" with or without my cooperation. I asked, "Please don't do this; please, please, please stop." He told me how sweet my hesitation was. "You know how sweet it will be in the morning when you realize you did want it. You'll be saying please differently and be glad you stayed. Or if not, I don't really care."

Numerous times during the night I tried to excuse myself to the bathroom and was told he wasn't done yet. He'd mount me again three or four times during the night. No alternative positions, no bondage of physical restraint. The psychological restraints and restrictions were significant. He was such an ugly human soul, such an animal. About four in the morning, he nudged me out of a fitful sleep. I had brought tears to my eyes as I thought he was going to sexually assault me again.

I didn't sob. I didn't cry out. I just let the tears roll down my cheeks as he straddled me but then he noticed. He went limp. He lost his erection. He said, "I'm done with you. How pathetic you are. How much more fun it would have been if you had allowed yourself to enjoy the night." I was told to let myself out. He called from the bedroom that I'd best not tell anyone where I'd been or what I'd done all night. I don't remember grabbing my clothes or dressing to leave. I do remember my hand on the doorknob and thinking: *just like that he's letting me go.* I don't remember the drive home or cleaning up and getting into my bed in the barracks. But all those things had to have happened. I must have been functional but it's all a dense fog. In [recalling my] capture the horror remains. In [my] regained freedom, I am numb.

In fear of my career, in fear of my safety, in fear of prison, I told no one. I'd have to face this alone. So I promised the little girl inside me that we'd put this away and come back to it one day when we were stronger. I just didn't know it would be 40 years later.

After that night a week passed, then a few weeks more. I waited for a call from NISO. No calls came. My calls to NISO weren't returned. I never heard from Petty Officer "S.D." or anyone we knew in common. I'm unaware to this day if any investigation was founded or took place at all after the two investigators interviewed me together. Had it already been concluded when the investigator who victimized me took over as my contact? Is that when the grooming began? I know my information was accurate. I know I did the right thing. I would not change the path I took to report the drug activity.

The words of that night stick with me, I think, because at that moment I thought they might be the last words I heard and I wanted to tell God as soon as I got to heaven. I still hear the words in my head when some phrase, a moment or a memory sets me off.

There is connectivity to that night. I remember it in flashes and snapshots yet other pieces of it are lost time where I can't remember at all. I can't recall the things I want to and I can't forget the things I don't want to recall. I cannot remember the agent's name for anything, not his heritage or ethnicity or his accent. His words are stuck in my head so clearly but his voice is not clear to me. Why not? I remember so many other trivial details. Does the trivial protect me from the significant? Is the little girl inside me holding back details to spare me?

The recollection of this horrible episode has been pushed down inside of me. I questioned what I could've done differently. At what point in the contact I had with this investigator could I have done something, anything to have headed this off? Even more so, [on] the night it all went bad what could I have done to have brought a better outcome? I still question myself. I still do and I get a big fat "SO WHAT?" from inside my head. So why do I still allow him to have power over my thoughts and why am I taking responsibility for his behavior? It can't be undone.

I found myself trusting nearly no one and protecting those I could trust. I protected the little girl inside me that felt all the ugliness of the world. I promised *her* we'd address it one day. As if doing anything differently would have those who mattered thinking less of me for it.

By remembering, I hope it makes it less damaging and less remembered. In the 40 years that passed, it is neither.

[1]My brother Neil gave me his permission in writing, to allow me to speak of him and identify him by name in this book.

[2]Commander Alvin Marsh gave me his permission, face-to-face and in writing, to allow me to speak of him and identify him by name in this book.

An Odd Occurrence
Desperate Conversations

Working alone on the eve watch (3:00 p.m. to 11:00 p.m.), I remember feeling quite pleased with myself, almost smug at my burgeoning career, as it was an honor to have such a level of trust and proficiency placed on my shoulders. There I was in a billet usually filled by those much more senior to my rank with far more years of experience or seniority than I had at that time.

At about 2100hrs, (9:00 p.m.), in the darkness of the radar room, the sudden clatter of the heavy enameled phone made me nearly jump out of my skin. The startling noise cut through the darkness and silence, hoisting me back to reality.

Somehow, with no encouragement or invitation from me, my ghosts of Cuba had come back to haunt me via the duty phone.

I snapped to, with a salute in my voice, and spoke with authority, "ATC/Boredom Control, Petty Officer Madden speaking. May I help you Sir?" I was the first female ever to be the voice of "Boredom Control" (the call sign for our division of air controllers). I was proud of that. I took it very seriously.

My professional demeanor was responded to by a very meek female voice, asking, "Diane, is that you?"

I replied, "Mom? Are you all right?" My mom was the only non-military person I'd ever given this telephone number.

The caller again asked, "Diane?"

"Yes, it's me. Mom, are you okay?"

Then in a much stronger voice, she said, "This isn't your mother. It's "D's" wife."

The evil specter of "D" had returned from the graveyard of my past in the form of a disembodied voice drifting through the long distance airwaves. I was furious! "How did you get this number? I am on duty! I have planes in the air. I cannot be talking to you!" I slammed the receiver into its cradle with such force it rattled everything near the desk, including me. I slumped into the chair and sat staring at the phone in disbelief.

Crap! Dammit! This cannot be happening. I will not allow this sewage to seep out of my past and into my new beginning.

I couldn't indulge thoughts of any of this. I had aircraft off the ground, under my control. The past needed to stay in the past. *Crap. Crap. Crap.*

With my birds all safely tucked back on deck, on the ground no longer flying, I was graced with only a brief moment to think before the ringing of the duty phone broke the silence once again.

Through the receiver came the same unnerving voice, "It's "D's" wife."

"Please don't call this number," I replied firmly but politely.

"Talk to me now or I'll be talking to your CO."

You Bitch! I wanted so much to say it—it was just below the surface about to escape when I heard myself actually say, "Ma'am, I only have an hour left on my watch. Can we finish this in less than that?" Having my birds in the nest, I could manage this now.

I quietly awaited her response and then she spoke. "Yes. Will you listen to me and hear me out? I'd like to finish this tonight."

I saw the wisdom in letting her do most of the talking and resolved that I would do as little of it on my end as possible. I simply said, "Talk."

She pointedly asked me to please stay away from "D". Before she had barely finished the sentence, I told her that the last time I saw "D" I was standing next to her in the Norfolk military air terminal. Clearly, I had hit a nerve as her tone of voice changed.

Sounding thoroughly agitated, she barked, "He's been at NAS JAX many times in the last two weeks to see you."

"Listen, I told you I haven't seen him. Where are you two stationed now?"

She responded as if I should know. "We're at Naval Station Mayport."

My heart sank. They were less than 10 miles from NAS JAX. *Crap. Crap. Crap.*

Parting the deafening silence, the softer tone of her,

"Hello? Are you still there?" let me know she was processing what I had just told her.

I responded, "Yes, I'm still here."

The agitation was gone from her voice and now she just sounded pathetic. "Please stay away from "D". He's my husband. I need him. Do you hear me?" She was now reduced to pleading for my cooperation in a situation I no longer had any part in, and I found myself feeling more annoyed than sympathetic.

At this point, I thought I had better choose my words carefully. In a monotone voice, I flatly said, "I'm listening. Can I say something yet?"

She then proceeded to lecture me about how I could start by explaining myself and why I couldn't stay away from her husband. I'd had just about enough when I decided I needed to take control of the situation. "Oh my dear girl; I listened to *you*, now will you hear *me* out?"

I mentally ran down my options. *Do I go for the throat? Do I release all my anger and pain? Do I plead with her to keep him away from me?* The answer came to me so clearly. She had no justifiable access to my feelings or emotions; therefore, I wasn't going to share any of them with the wife of my predator. Lashing out at her from beneath the armor that guarded my anger wasn't going to serve me well. There would be no joy in destroying this wounded animal of a woman.

Apparently, my silence stretched out too long. She spoke first. "I said I'd listen, so go ahead and talk." There was that condescending tone of hers rising once again.

I could feel I was getting my Irish up. *She* was going to take an attitude with *me?* I wasn't having it. It was all I could do to maintain a professional demeanor, knowing I might have to defend my actions following tonight. Regardless, I opened up and spoke my peace.

"First off, I didn't know you and your family were anywhere in the area. I haven't seen "D" since Norfolk. He may have been coming to NAS JAX the past two weeks to see me but he hasn't found me. I don't want to see him. I don't want to talk to him. I don't want him in my life in any way whatsoever! Do I make myself clear?"

Swimming in her neurosis, she still had to ask, "So you aren't seeing my "D"?"

Once again, I repeated to her emphatically, "NO! I am not, nor do I want to. I am sorry for what this has done to your marriage, but it is *your* marriage and none of my concern."

She sighed. "So you *will* stay away then?"

Is this woman not hearing me? Is she so desperate to hold together her poor excuse of a marriage that she thinks that calling me is going to help her do that?

Once again, she grasped through the awkward silence with, "Hello? Are you still there?"

"Listen to me," I said with authority, "I'm going to stop him from ever coming back to NAS Jacksonville to see me. Will you feel better then and never call me again?"

She was quick to query, "How will you do that? You can't stop him."

I had officially had it with this woman. I snapped. "Don't think for a moment that I can't! I can! I will! Are we done here?"

With that, the meek voice that first called me was back. "I hope so. I love "D"."

Although my verbal response was, "Good for you," my actual thought in true Navy form was - *Sounds like a personal problem and not my problem.*

My mid-watch duty sailor relieved me of the watch. My shift was over. I maintained my military bearing. As I reported, "no unusual traffic or occurrence during my shift," I signed out of the duty log and went back to the crib (my room at the barracks).

Lying in my rack (my bed) with only my thoughts, I reasoned my way through exactly how I was going to stop "D" from ever stepping foot on NAS JAX again. My first instinct was to call my brother, Neil, in Cuba. I imagined his response would be something along the lines of "Handle your shit sailor." Better I should tell him over a cold beer years later after it was "handled." I still owe him that beer. I don't remember ever telling him.

I wanted no fallout from my past life or regrets to taint

my new more promising life. "D's" wife threatened to tell my CO (Commanding Officer). Well, better he not be blindsided. I would seek him out and tell him first. I rationalized myself into potentially very dangerous territory.

I sought out the division command officer the next day. This was a major infraction of jumping the chain of command. I'd been accused of doing this more than a few times and had, in fact, done it far too often to plead ignorance if busted for it again. I took on a dangerous attitude of "No guts! No glory!" To hell or be damned; I did it anyway.

Upon being granted a hearing, the first thing out of my mouth was the acknowledgment of my obvious infraction and of my desire to continue regardless of consequence. I asked for a get-out-of-jail-free card so if it was deemed I was too far out of line I might withdraw my request. It was something of a tentative approach, but effective.

The CO actually chuckled at my preemptive apology. He encouraged me to continue at my own peril, almost as a challenge. No guts. No glory. This may not have been a well-reasoned advance.

I told him I wanted absolutely no one in my immediate division to know any of the backstory or how it had come to this.

Years later, I look back with laughter at my naïve and foolish belief that they didn't already know. I hadn't wised up enough yet to realize this boys club *all* knew, which was why I was such a blind target. I underestimated my enemy due to my inexperience. As I progressed in my career I came to learn how the game was played, but for then I was still vulnerable.

I unloaded on the CO. I told him every nasty detail since I was boots-on-the-ground in Cuba. He himself admitted it was far more than I could be expected to handle alone. In the same resolute tone with which I had told "D's" wife I would stop her husband from stepping foot on NAS JAX, the CO now assured me, "It stops today." Oddly enough, I had the same question that she had posed now rolling around in my mind. *How?* I was smart enough not to ask it aloud. All that mattered was the CO had the rank to make it happen.

I walked out of the Admiral's office in the Air Wings building, nearly trembling. I was sure anyone who made eye contact with me was going to know I'd just broken at least four Articles of the UCMJ (Uniform Code of Military Justice).

As was promised, the unauthorized visits ceased immediately. I was led to understand there was a tel-con (telephone conversation) which took place between my CO and the CO at Naval Station Mayport. Although I should have left it alone, I couldn't resist. I checked with base police. I learned a "No Access" order had been given restricting "D" from entering NAS JAX.

The WAVE who had been ordered to connect the call between the two CO's roomed down the hall from me in the barracks. She thought I'd like to know the call had been made. I could only hope she hadn't told others so willingly or as quickly as she hurried to tell me.

Decades later, I saw her at a veterans gathering outside Chicago. I wondered whom else she'd might have told of my visit or the resulting action taken that day. It must've been all over my face. Enough so that she came right up to me, hugged me and whispered, "Honor among WAVES. I told no one."

My past, again, for now remained in my past. Another promise made to the young girl who suffered so much. *Now is not the time. Not yet. But someday. Be patient. But for now it all needs to remain a secret.*

Incident #5

January 1976 to July 1976 - NAS Jacksonville, FL

I was stationed at NAS Jacksonville from September 1974 until October 1976. My brother, Neil (AC1 Madden) joined me at NAS JAX for brother/sister duty. He and I secured off-base housing on Lake Shore Blvd, off Blanding, approximately 30 minutes from the base. We shared a three-bedroom upstairs of a house on the St. John's River. We rented from an elderly couple, "L" and his wife. Neil and I shared my vehicle. I worked day-watch (7 a.m. to 3 p.m.) and Neil worked eve-watch (3 p.m. to 11 p.m.). I'd get a ride to the base. [Neil would] drive my car in. I'd drive it home and he'd get a ride home at end of watch. It worked out. Life had taken on a happy domestication and a comfortable rhythm of family life. We took care of each other and made a nice home: a safe harbor.

I had rationalized away the entire experience with NISO as my own bad judgment (again) and the consequences of being a bad judge of character. I'd been gullible and foolish with "S.D.'s" drug dealings, trusting and having faith in NISO, and blamed myself for any fallout. The nightmares stopped after a time but, every so often, they vividly reappeared. I never did tell Neil about the NISO agent, so we never went after the agent to settle accounts. What was the point? The threats of the agent were still fresh in my memory. I didn't want to call his bluff.

My resolve to put the NISO incident behind me was reflected in my performance evaluations. It was noted that I was the only Seaman SN (E-3) and the only WAVE in a group of E-6s and E-7s and in the Remarks section it stated, "She has a cheerful manner with a smile and hello for everyone regardless of her feelings or personal problems."

I suspected they all knew I was emotionally damaged from Cuba and Portsmouth, but they gave me an environment in which to excel and serve. I continued to focus on my duty assignment. As much as I was trying to remain professional, Senior Chief "Madrid" was a constant challenge. I reported to him in my division. I continued to deflect his

51

advances. I refused to engage in any misconduct while maintaining my focus on my career.

As stated in my evaluation dated "**31 Jan 76** to **31 Jul 76**," my reassignment from Radar Stander/Radar Controller to the full time Statistical Data Analyst was at my request because I excelled in the field. I knew my reports and analysis were valued and read by numerous senior officers. It was noted that much of the data I provided was used in decision-making summits attended by high-ranking Navy personnel. I was not going to be shy or apologetic about my skills.

I no longer wanted to report to Sr. Chief "Madrid" because of his constant harassment and unwanted advances. Sr. Chief "Madrid" wrote negative remarks on my performance evaluations. He referenced my behavior as "shifting from liberated female versus using [her] femininity to [her] best advantage as [she] saw the need in an effort to achieve [her] personal agenda." There was never any doubt for me, and others would soon come to realize, this was a result of my denying his persistent sexual advances.

I needed a final performance appraisal attesting to my worthiness for Recruiting Duty. Sr. Chief "Madrid" wrote my appraisal, and in preparing to give me the oral review of my evaluation, he asked the division Lieut. Cdr. (LCDR) "H" to sit in on it because it was so negative and reflected a drop in my overall performance numbers.

I was told by LCDR "H" that Sr. Chief "Madrid" wanted a witness there to verify I'd been counseled. I listened in absolute silence, growing angry, scared, and praying for courage. I listened carefully to the verbal reprimand I was given. I fought my impulse to shut down. There was no way I was going to give "Madrid" the satisfaction of my tears. I had to detach and stay neutral. Familiar territory for me. If we were going to go to war, here and now, then I needed to stay engaged and devoid of all emotion. LCDR "H" asked if I had anything to say for myself. His voice was monotone and accusatory at the same time.

"Can this be a no-ranks conversation? Can I speak freely?"

I was told rank and respect was in order but to speak openly.

I began, "With all due respect . . ." (This is a safety net phrase [known throughout the Navy] to blanket a statement that might be seen as disrespectful. Truthfully, at this point I didn't know how it was going to go or what I was going to say.) I went on to state I actually welcomed the presence of the Lt. Commander. I was relieved he was there. I fully acknowledged my understanding of what had been leveled against me. I asked if we could examine more closely the decline in my numbers and the origins of the changes.

I was granted this request and told to speak freely. I unloaded every sexual advance, every unwelcomed kiss, grope and grab, every inappropriate act of Chief "Madrid", whether in uniform, on-duty or after hours in civilian clothes, and my ultimate denial of sexual intercourse which I felt in large part prompted the bad performance appraisal. Both men looked like I hit them with a brick to the face. My heart sank. I was sure I'd pay the price for my candor.

LCDR "H" regained his composure. He asked Sr. Chief "Madrid", "Is what she is saying true?" I was more than surprised when "Madrid" admitted to all of it. Was he just so sure there'd be no consequences or was he proud of his actions? I couldn't tell. There was a long silence. I willed myself not to be the first to speak.

LCDR "H" asked what I sought as the resolution to this appraisal's unexpected outcome. I said I wanted our division CO to be made aware but no disciplinary action taken which would harm Sr. Chief "Madrid's" wife and three kids or cause them to be aware of what he'd done. His paygrade could have been cut. His paycheck could have been reduced. I felt badly for his family. His wife was so sweet and thought the sun rose and set in this man. He was a hero to his kids. I wasn't going to shatter their world. I had babysat their children. My brother and I had been to his home for barbecues. He had a beautiful family, which he had now put in jeopardy. It seemed I had more concern for his family's well-being than he did. I wanted no action taken which would have a lasting effect on his career, which would thereby affect his family. I also wanted to never report to him again in the chain of command. Lastly, I wanted a new appraisal by someone other than Sr. Chief "Madrid".

Our CO, CDR "A" was told of it. He asked me nothing more than, "Are you good with it?" A week or so later he asked if I was doing okay, and that was enough for me. CDR "A" let me know he knew. I said to let it alone. I'd fight my own battles. I'd be gone in a few weeks, off to recruiting school. This was awkward because CDR "A" was my ride to work each morning so my brother and I could share a vehicle. In fact, it had been CDR "A" who'd come up with the transportation scheduling idea because he cared enough to be concerned for his sailors' family situations. All those morning rides in, I'd never jumped the chain of command as I was so often accused of (and too often had done) but I had never done so regarding this topic. I think he respected I hadn't as he now knew I could have many times brought it up on any given morning. I was trying to handle my own career. I felt I had professionally risen above the fray.

Sr. Chief "Madrid" was the most senior enlisted and I was the least ranked sailor as an E-4. I no longer reported to him so I steered clear of him in avoidance. I remained respectful and professional when our paths crossed but I tried to be sure that they didn't. My acceptance to Enlisted Naval Recruiter Orientation (ENRO) was approved. I was to report to Orlando **2 Oct 76**. The whole division was supportive of me achieving this goal—all but one. I certainly understood why.

In mid-September [1976], I was home alone while my brother, Neil, was on duty. Sr. Chief "Madrid" showed up at the home I shared with Neil. The upstairs of the house Neil and I shared had an outside separate stairwell private entrance. I heard a huge thudding noise like something crashing in the corner of the house.

54

Our elderly landlord couple lived on the 1st floor. When I heard the thud, my first thought was that "L" had needed something and fell down the stairs coming to get me. As I recall it, I wasn't afraid as I was rushing to rescue "L". I threw open the door thinking I'd fly down the stairs to help him. Just as I opened the door, there at the top of the stairs was a very drunk, very angry Sr. Chief "Madrid".

He pushed his way in. He yelled at me for calling him out during my performance review. He was angry [that] CDR "A" knew what he'd done. I pointed out to him it had been his own bad behavior which had gotten him in trouble. I was not to be blamed for putting an end to it. I pushed the point by stating I'd lessened the punishment he was due by offering my resolution so perhaps he should be grateful. This was clearly not what he came for and not what he wanted to hear. I'd not been told what his punishment was but now I knew some of it. Sr. Chief "Madrid" blurted out in slurred speech "You had no trouble sleeping with a married man in Cuba and killing his baby."

So there it was. They had all known of my mistake/misfortune or mishap—I still don't know how to define what happened to me, what was done to me in Cuba but they did all know about it. I would've been happy to leave Jacksonville without confirmation of who knew what about me. But "Madrid" couldn't even give me that.

Sr. Chief "Madrid" was so drunk and menacing. In a flash, I was thinking how well the others in my division handled knowing of Cuba. It was noted in my evaluation dated "**14 Sep 74** to **28 Feb 75**" how I had not let personal tragedy affect my military performance. I initially resented seeing that notation and wondered what it was referencing but, as I had suspected all along, they had known. Now this drunken pig was throwing it in my face.

I lost it. I wanted to kill him and the NISO agent and "D" from Cuba and the MAA female in the barracks at NS Norfolk. I snapped. I started defending myself with all the pent-up rage going back to day one. I didn't know I was capable of such hatred. When Sr. Chief "Madrid" pushed his way into the house, throwing me up against the wall, I was done being anybody's victim. I came back swinging. Every raw emotion I'd pushed down was raging now. I knocked him off his feet and tried to run to the phone.

I got as far as the living room when he lunged at me. He spun me around and shoved me toward the couch where I fell over the arm of it. My brother and I had this boxy, hard-armed couch with wooden caps on the tops of the armrests.

As I fell back over the arm of the couch, my lower back smacked the wooden armrest hard. My torso made a horrible cracking noise, like the branch of a tree snapping. We both heard it crack. I screamed in pain. He sobered up immediately. He didn't ask if I was okay or offer to get me help. He just stood there staring at me. I screamed for him to get the hell out. He ran out and down the same stairs he couldn't walk up when he'd arrived unannounced only minutes earlier. I couldn't stand up or walk. I laid there for what seemed like forever. I knew Neil would be home about 2330hrs (11:30 p.m.) I had to pull it together before he saw me.

I had some goofy thoughts as I lay on the floor waiting for the pain to pass. I remember thinking I was not going to let "Madrid" ruin my getting Recruiting Duty. If I called the police, then there would be a civilian criminal report because we lived off-base, and then the Military Police report, and all the hearings and proceedings involved in both. NISO would have to get involved and I had no faith in them. Cuba taught me cops cannot be trusted. (How ironic I ended up with a 20-year career in law enforcement and a full pension.) It would just delay me going to recruiter's school, and isn't that what "Madrid" was trying to do to me all along? I may have been the one on the ground injured, but "Madrid" was not going to win.

My big plan was to keep my mouth shut and heal up. As I recall, it was a weekend. I had days off ahead of me. I'd let "Madrid" worry if I was going to turn him in for retaliation. Let him sweat it. I'd never speak of it again. Put it behind me. I played it off to my brother when he got home. I told him goofy Sr. Chief "Madrid" showed up drunk and I had to throw him out. No big deal. Done. But I wasn't healing up. I needed medical attention. By early in the week, I gave up and went to sick call. It was **21 Sep 76.** I said I'd fallen three days prior at the base swimming pool. On **18 Sep 76** I did actually fall at the pool; it was an accident. Hitting the same place in my back caused me to be reinjured. Now I could explain my bruises. The Corpsman seemed suspicious of the advanced stages of bruising, but he was more concerned for my well-being than the actual source and timeline of my injury.

After everything that jerk did to sabotage me, I lied to get help and he was going to get a pass on the attack. I did it for me, not him. I needed to heal up and move on.

In less than two weeks, I was to report to ENRO (Enlisted Naval Recruiting Orientation) in Orlando for five weeks followed by a two-week leave. I didn't lie to protect Sr. Chief "Madrid"—it was to save myself. I wasn't going to let anything or anyone derail me. I was doing the wrong thing for the right reason.

I was able to push it down with another promise to the little girl to revisit it someday and make sense of it then. But for now, we had to keep it a secret.

I just wanted to be gone from NAS Jacksonville. I was focused forward toward giving 100% to my newest challenge - Navy recruiting. I knew I gave NAS JAX a strong effort in spite of it all. My evaluations were testament to my skills and professionalism.

But here I was, once again, face-to-face with the pervasive attitude stemming from this culture of acceptance of sexually demeaning behaviors which were part of the fabric of the Navy. I did not like my violent outburst and response to Sr. Chief "Madrid". It was out of character. Or so I thought. It stunned me to see what level of rage I was capable of summoning up from within me. Perhaps the little girl inside me had a bit of the banshee about her.

Nearly 40 years later, I realize it wasn't my fault. Yet it was, in part, because my way of handling it didn't stop it there and then. I worked around it to enable myself to be a productive sailor and a contributing asset to the Navy.

[Being] selected for Navy recruiting was an honor. It was required I have two letters of recommendation from commissioned officers. LCDR "M.B." was my division LCDR. His letter is dated **10 Jun 76**. LCDR "S.W." swore me in for my re-enlistment **1 Sept 76**. His letter dated **8 Jun 76**.

I was seriously determined to go forward but clearly I had aged from the bright-eyed, all-hopes-for-the-future kid who was in boot camp in the summer of 1973. I see such a look of resignation in my face, ironically just as I am re-enlisting for more of the same (abuse). At the very moment that photograph was being taken, I was computing how many more times would I face MST if I were to stay in the Navy 20 years. My military bearing carried the day.

Selection to recruiting also required a face-to-face interview and appraisal by the base captain. Captain "B" interviewed me on **10 Jun 76**. I mention this because it reaffirms what I experienced while at NAS Jacksonville. It speaks to the level at which the Navy information pipeline operated to the detriment of the women.

On the Interviewer's Appraisal Sheet, Captain "B" observed me to be "forthright" and "mature." In the narrative he said, "She is mature in her outlook." Reading the summary of the interview made me feel better about myself than I had in a long time. I feel it is important to share the content of the interview briefly to clearly show the atmosphere.

The interview started quite comfortably. We chatted almost casually as we settled into a relaxed conversation. Then, out of the blue, he sprung it on me. In a very direct tone and under his direct gaze he said, "So exactly what happened in Cuba? Summarize your behavior." I had the passing thought, *Oh God, he knows too. Is there anyone in this command or in the whole damn Navy that doesn't know the horrors of what happened in Cuba and Portsmouth?*

I tried to maintain my composure. I felt gut punched but tried not to flinch. I decided to be 100% truthful with him as graphically as I could explain. It wasn't malicious compliance and I had a respectful posture and volume to my voice. I took full ownership, as I left nothing out of the horror I'd experienced. With what remaining pride I had left, I summarized by saying, "I had wanted to play the games the big kids played and I got caught with my bloomers down, Sir." I wanted my meaning to be clear but in a lady-like manner. I assured him it would not happen again—not in recruiting, not ever in my life again. So it became clear to me even the Commanding Officer of the Air Wing of the Atlantic Fleet knew about GITMO too. He knew the answer before he asked the question. Good life lesson there for me.

His assessment of me for the recruiting Interview Appraisal Sheet (NavPers 1100/18) read "mature in her outlook," "forthright" and "I most strongly recommend her selection." I feel my utter and complete candor led to his summation of my character.

Oddly enough, the day after I met with Captain "B" for my interview, he became Vice Admiral "B". He was playfully kind when I saw him weeks later and he asked, "Would you have been so candid, so forthright, if [you'd] known [you were] telling an Admiral about [your] misadventure in Cuba?" He meant it as encouragement to continue to be honest and forthright regardless of rank. He'd told my brother, Neil, of our meeting and the outcome, weeks later when they joined up as doubles partners for the base tennis team. It made Neil proud of me and we laughed about Cuba for the first time. I wasn't offended by Admiral "B" because he was right in all aspects. He had referenced a sexual event of my life but not in an offensive manner. He was respectful and not demeaning. His leadership was as much about his actions as his words.

It proved to be sage guidance and served me well in the performance appraisal Sr. Chief "Madrid" had LCDR "H" sit in on. It gave me courage to speak up and be forthright regardless of rank.

The final piece of the package needed for recruiting was a special transfer evaluation from CMDR "G" [who was] the Air Wing and Terminal Commanding Officer. The evaluation covered the timeframe of **1 Feb 76** to **1 Oct 76**. The evaluation showed my marks returning to the level of 3.8s and one 3.6 with a strong narrative explanation of my performance and skills. The timeframe negated Sr. Chief "Madrid's" evaluation and sexist remarks almost completely. (Although something told me to hold on to "Madrid's" biased review just in case, and I'm glad I did.) More importantly, I was told CMDR "G" wanted to do his part to correct a wrong against me and wanted me evaluated fairly on merit and my record. The evaluation was dated **20 Sep 76** and signed. It was the appraisal I had requested when I exposed Sr. Chief "Madrid". All my requests for the outcome had been granted.

[On] **2 Oct 76** I reported to ENRO.

There are no pictures of my military life after Jacksonville. There was nothing more I wanted to remember about the military. [In the] timeline of [my] declining happiness spanning 1973 through 1976, with each incident of MST the light in my eyes dimmed a bit more.

[Bye-bye NAS Jacksonville!]

Incident #6
23 Nov 76 to December 1976 -
Navy Recruiting District Chicago

Recruiting school was sheer camaraderie start to finish. It made me regain hope the actual recruiting duty would build the same bonds.

I was going to have an apartment in West Chicago paid for by the Navy. 310A Wilson Street. I could be in my hometown *and* be in the Navy. Safe at last, with personal peril no longer a constant and conscious concern in my daily living, I could really dig into my career.

I got to NRD (Naval Recruiting District) Chicago on **23 Nov 76**. I was assigned to the Wheaton office. Despite it being the community surroundings I'd grown up in, I was not a successful addition at my new assignment. DuPage County, Illinois, was affluent and saw itself as elite—socially and culturally above military service. In 1976, Wheaton was a college-bound town of affluent households and spoiled brats. I didn't really want any of them in my Navy.

Shortly after being assigned to NRD Chicago, I became suspicious of my fellow recruiters when I heard of a meeting being held at the Lawrence & Milwaukee recruiting office one evening. I'd asked to be transferred there previously to improve my chances of succeeding. The Jefferson Park neighborhood had a strong work ethic. The recruit pool consisted of the sons and daughters of immigrants. It felt suspicious when I was told *not* to attend the meeting as I was "too new" [at] recruiting for it to be beneficial. It was early December 1976.

It seemed to me, since I was so new to the job, I should go. I could learn from their experience. How could I still have been so naïve, after all that I'd been through?

Something just did not add up so I decided to spy on them at their meeting. I snuck in the back door of the recruiting station's building. I hid in the stockroom area to eavesdrop on the meeting. A new sales incentive contest was being announced. Sales meant body count or enlistees to meet recruiting goals. It required a $100 entry fee, winner take all. I was now intrigued and annoyed I'd been left out. I wasn't left out completely as it turned out. The incentive contest was "Who Can Nail Her First?" Obvious benefits of sex for the winner but also the entry fee pot and braggin' rights. Just as I was about to show myself, someone said, "According to GITMO, she only does married men so no single guys." I never showed myself. I left my hiding place heartbroken and drove back out to West Chicago in tears.

It was going to be no different. Before I left the recruiters' meeting, I had heard eight guys out of a room of about 20 recruiters get in on the contest. Once I'd stopped crying, I knew I was going to get even. I just didn't know how yet. So I waited to see what the days ahead would bring. I wondered who would be active in their efforts to win, who had been pressured into entry, and who had been the eight to enter the contest?

Five of them hit the ground running. The offers of love and devotion, sex and seduction, horseplay, and the utmost secrecy and discretion were almost flattering had I not known the origins of their newfound passion-filled lust for me.

I resolved to beat them at their own game. I scripted what I would say to them and be sure to say the same thing to each when alone for our moments. I'd borrowed money from each of them for no good reason other than to create a bond of proof. I ultimately gave each of them an apartment key for late night visits but made them promise to call first so I could make myself ready for them. Only a few made the effort to come to the apartment but all of them willingly took the key. Three of them never made themselves known to me. I actually thought more of them for putting the money in for the entry fee just to reduce peer pressure but never intending to act on it. The active five were falling all over themselves, each of them thinking they were advancing. I was exhausted with all the ego feeding I was doing.

A few of them even came by my apartment hoping to win the incentive but none ever did. None of them ever needed to use their key because I met them at the door. I [later heard] they were bragging about having been out to my apartment.

On the day the incentive contest was over, there was another recruiters' meeting I was told *not* to attend. I appeared to be relieved not to have to go. What did I know anyway? They didn't think I knew about the first one. But I did attend via the same access as before.

As the boys started comparing notes, offering intimate conversations as proof of conquest, they all began to realize they'd been told all the same lines of sweet nothings from me. I wish I could have seen their faces—not just the participants but the uninvolved recruiters too. The tone of the room and the voices in the room changed. The recruiter who'd been thought *most-likely-to-nail-her* (me) blurted out, "But I got a key to her apartment!" (As though he possessed the trophy proof.) But, then the four others also produced a key.

Just as they all started to realize they'd been had, I came out of the stockroom carrying a shoe box. The room gasped. I had their full attention when I said, "Whose wife do I call first?" Then I opened my shoebox and produced one guy's belt, another guy's watch, the Italian guy's golden horn necklace and cross [to be clear, I am not speaking about my nice Italian Corpsman] and, best of all, for the most-likely-to-succeed candidate, I produced his wedding band.

I repeated my question. "Whose wife do I call first?" No response [came]. I said, "By the way, none of you will be getting back the money you loaned me and I will be taking the $800 pot." I asked if the gentlemen in the room would clearly agree I had won.

One of them asked if I wanted my apartment key back as the others all had them out and ready to return to me. I smiled as I told them [that might] be someone's apartment key but it never fit the lock on my apartment door. I suggested they keep them as a reminder not to fuck with me again. Had I lowered myself to their level or was it just leverage to protect myself?

[Today], I vacillate between thinking it was not my finest hour and that perhaps indeed it was.

In the spring, we had a division barbecue at the Italian guy's house. All families of the recruiters, kids included, attended. I came alone. I wore a T-shirt with song lyrics printed on the front.

"You didn't have to love me like ya' did but ya' did and I thank you."

Each of the incentive participants squirmed uneasily for the afternoon as I circulated among their families and the other more honorable recruiters. Then one of the wives approached me saying the shirt I was wearing was a maternity shirt and "Oh my God! Are you pregnant?" She was all happy and bubbly and gushy. I watched a few of the guys get really nervous. I loved it and maybe let them freak out a little too long. Finally, I said how embarrassed I was and that I just liked the song and 'oh gosh no, no babies here.' Just a reminder to the boys—*I can play nasty anytime, anywhere one of you gets out of line again.* It was almost too easy but so effective.

None of the recruiters across any of the branches tried to get over on me again. It was almost an air of acceptance at joining in their sanctioned bad behavior and prevailing over them.

I served at the Wheaton office from **23 Nov 76** until **31 Jan 77**. I moved to the infamous recruiting station at Lawrence and Milwaukee on **1 Feb 77** until **31 Jul 77**. My transfer to Lawrence and Milwaukee got approved. Remarks were made in fun about me knowing the ins and outs of the building already. I took it as a sign they still felt the sting of my payback. It was in their best interests not to cross me again and not to forget.

Even though my office location changed, I stayed in the West Chicago apartment because of the rental agreement. As military stationed within the community, we had no barracks. We were allotted civilian housing paid for directly from the Navy to the landlord. My military salary was not compatible with civilian rental costs. The drive was long but it put a nice distance between my Navy life and my home life.

A horrific incident took place in late March/early April 1977 at 310A Wilson St. causing me to relocate my residence closer to my Chicago office. I moved to Berteau Avenue near Irving Park Road and Kedzie Avenue (4800 North) in Chicago. Regardless of cost, finances were not a factor when my personal safety became at issue. I could no longer live in my apartment in West Chicago. **(See Incident #7)**

Incident #7

1 Feb 77 to 31 Jul 77 -
Navy Recruiting District Chicago
1 Aug 77 to 15 Dec 77 -
Transfer Granted - 536 South Clark
11 Nov 77 to 22 Feb 78 -
Great Lakes Naval Medical Center

While living at 310 A Wilson Street, West Chicago, my recruiting assignment had me reassigned to the Lawrence and Milwaukee Avenue Navy Recruiting office at 4800 North in the Jefferson Park area making my commute to the office just about an hour and a half by car. I didn't mind the time in the car. I rather enjoyed it.

Upon returning home from the office, I didn't realize I had forgotten a recruit's file at the station. I had to pick up recruits by 0430 but must be in possession of their files [in order] to be transporting them in the government vehicle.

Sometime in the late evening, approximately 9 p.m., there was an insistent knock at my apartment door. I yelled, "It is late. I can't open the door. Come back tomorrow." The voice on the other side yelled back, "Open the door Madden. You're gonna wanna see me." I recognized the voice of the USMC recruiter and didn't hesitate to open the door. He waved a recruit's folder at me and said something about how I'd need it in the morning so he saved me a trip back to the office.

I had been sure I'd packed it in my bag but there it was, in fact, one of mine. I was really obsessive in my preparedness but, oh well, I had it now. What did it matter? It occurred to me weeks later he had deliberately removed the file from my bag. I had forgotten my keys back in my office and left my bag unattended outside his office for just a moment while I went to retrieve the keys. It gave him opportunity. It gave him a reason to bring the file to me and gain access to my home.

At the time, I was just grateful to have the file. I thanked him for going so far out of his way and opened the door for him to leave. He called me a "goof" for my rookie mistake. He bent to kiss my forehead, like a big brother to a little sister. He stunk of stale beer and hard liquor. I asked whose car he'd driven. He was still in uniform. He said [he drove] his uncle's car, then chuckled and said, "Your uncle's car, ya' know? Uncle Sam's car, get it?" Great—a drunk's humor.

I told him I couldn't let him leave. He'd sleep on the couch. I got blankets, sheets and a pillow for him. I set him a bedroll on the couch. He was a complete gentleman even though he was clearly drunk. He was snoring before I even left the room. I went to my room, closed the door, checked the alarm was set, and was off to sleep.

About 1 a.m., as I slept facedown, I felt his weight on my back. I froze and then wiggled to get away. I told him, "Don't make it worse. Get off me. Don't! Don't! Don't!" Just as I took a big breath to use the exhale to try to throw him off me, he said in a whisper into my right ear, "Scream and I will snap your neck." I went limp and let him rape me. It was pointless to resist. He was very vigorous in his efforts of self-gratification and completely oblivious to my lifeless response. He finished. I said nothing. The alarm went off. I awoke alone in my apartment, alone in my heart, and alone in my emptiness.

Nothing was ever said of it; not between him and me; not me to the authorities. Please. The scandal in my hometown [and] across the military branches would have been such bad publicity for the military. My brother lived only six blocks away. I didn't want to shame him or our family in our hometown by drawing attention to such a lurid act. I had signed on for this life. He had not. It's odd for me to pass by that address now without remembering. The West Chicago Police Department sits just one block down on Spencer, though back in the '70s the Police Department was still uptown on McConnell. It was a world away from the reality of that night and out of reach. It wasn't even a question of reporting it. The attack—the rape—felt like it came with the territory. No good deed goes unpunished. I picked up my recruits and did my duty.

In the weeks that followed, I found it increasingly intolerable to be in my apartment. My brass bed that I'd saved up for and wanted my whole life was no longer my treasured sleep haven. I could not sleep in it ever again.

To this day, the sight of a brass bed triggers flashbacks. I still am well aware of where I am and who is there but after the initial startling, it's more of a daydreaming fog moment. I don't flip out. I just shut down as I remember it all at once and completely. It literally runs fast-forward through my mind.

Even with free rent and residence in my hometown, I had to find somewhere else to live. I had to move. I thought West Chicago would make the Navy a better, safer place for me, but instead the Navy made West Chicago worse and brought only ugly memories of my first apartment alone. I resigned myself to the acceptance I would never be safe. No man in my life to trust or love, in the military and facing a life of vigilance or victimization—no one anywhere could be trusted. Life was a very lonely place for me [as well as for] the little girl [inside my head]. But for now we would have to keep it a secret.

The increase in my alcohol consumption at the recruiting office after-hours made the trip in the dark out to West Chicago, drunk almost every night, a dangerously bad behavior. I even had the guy in the toll booth on I-88 keeping an anxious watch for me, and he said he worried about me as I passed through each night. I thought a lot about why I was drinking so much [and] how numb it made me feel. I tried to make sense of a senseless downward spiral. It was just easier to get drunk and not think.

I relocated to within a few blocks of the Lawrence and Milwaukee office. I had the approval to break the lease using the distance after transferring from the Wheaton office as a plausible reason. I didn't have to share the real reason behind the move. I was wising up enough to know no one was going to care anyway if I did expose the real reason for it. I truly felt some of the recruiters would think I had it coming for having prevailed over my fellow Navy recruiters.

My evaluations had gotten significantly better at Lawrence and Milwaukee. Three 3.8s, one 3.6 [and one] 3.4, with the Remarks section of me having "conquered initial adjustment problems." I often wondered if that remark referred to my dismal recruiting stats in Wheaton or my exceptional success in destroying the incentive contest of Incident #6.

Regardless, I was drinking far too much. I felt betrayed and alone. I had sent so many Marine wanna-be-soldiers to the USMC recruiter and he had given me many recruits better suited to the Navy than to the Marines. Professionally we had been respectful and admirable. I had initially thought he was so handsome and so honorable (and so far out of my reach) I now resented his fellow recruiters for not knowing what he'd done to me and what a hypocrite he was. But how would they know? I had not told them. I had not told anyone. So, I drank. I still recruited hard and heavy everyday but I was drinking just as hard and heavy every night.

How pathetic and damaged I'd become. Now, in addition to still having to see the USMC recruiter daily in the recruiting station, I had the financial burden of renting a civilian place on a military paycheck. I'd changed my residence and was near where Irving Park Road and Kedzie Avenue meet. I was living on Berteau Avenue in a basement. It wasn't bohemian chic. I couldn't play it off as remnants of my hippie-esque pre-Navy life. I ended up living in a depressing, musty basement apartment alone. Even my cat, Frazetta, ran off the first day. I didn't even go looking for her. I didn't blame her. I didn't want to be there either.

I knew I needed to end the daily pressure of seeing the USMC recruiter at the office. There was the constant fear of ever being the only two in the office and what would happen to me if that happened. I feared he would take my silence following the attack as permission to revisit me.

Even though I was doing good work at Lawrence and Milwaukee, I told my Chief I could do even better with a transfer to 536 South Clark in downtown Chicago to work for Chief "B.K."

1 Aug 77 to 15 Dec 77 - Transfer Granted - 536 South Clark

Just as I said I would, I delivered. I earned a Gold Wreath for recruiting excellence in the 3rd quarter of 1977 for recruiting an average of eight bodies a month. One month we had 15. I had an outstanding evaluation—all 3.8s. There was talk of making me Sailor of the Year. Thanks but no thank you.

But other recruiters were asking me if I'd forgotten any files lately? Was the pressure getting to me? Did I need a designated driver? When we were gathered in groups, all branches, at the induction center (AFEES) someone would ask, "Should I nudge ya' when I get up or just let myself out?" *USMC PIG!* I had kept quiet about his (the Marine recruiter's) "conduct unbecoming" and he launched a bragging rights rumor. I was so relieved I had moved from the apartment and told no one my new address. I had many nights of fearing he'd come back, or perhaps even one of his buddies he may have told might show up on my doorstep. It made me even more [certain] I was right to have moved regardless of the financial hardship and dismal living conditions.

It was ironic to hear the phrase, *'Should I nudge ya' when I get up?'* On one of my first days in recruiting, Chief "B.K." had said that very thing to me in the Wheaton office in front of everyone. I stood up and sashayed suggestively right up to him and slapped his face to make the ground rules crystal clear. It had. I got his immediate respect and no disciplinary charges. Someone in the room warned me I should be careful because I might end up working for Chief "B.K." one day; and that did come to pass. The big difference was that from day one, Chief "B.K." was a straight shooter who, while he enjoyed women extensively, respected them and admired them. He gave me every opportunity to excel in my career and exceed all expectations. As it turns out, he was quite impressed by how I had outmaneuvered the sales incentive program and its participants. He said it was then he knew I was someone to be reckoned with. I took that as high praise. But [whenever I] heard other sleazy recruiters asking whether they should *nudge me when they get up or just let themselves out,* that same phrase had a new ugliness to it. It sickened me. I didn't react at all to the taunt of the recruiters who said it. I figured the little boys would tire of the game if it didn't get the desired response.

As we headed into the fall [season] of 1977, Chief "B.K." remarked I'd lost my spirit for the job. I had. I gave up. I didn't have a fight left in me. I couldn't do my job. I didn't feel safe out in the dark at 0330. Yet I felt safer there than in the company of military personnel. I'd self-talk, warning myself to snap out of it. Deal with it by setting it aside for now. Come back to it later. Do the job [I] committed to do.

But I had given up. I just kept expecting to be jumped in surroundings where I'd never felt tentative or unsafe before. It was hopeless. There was no safe place in my life. How many more attacks or rapes, episodes of verbal or physical abuse should I expect to come? How many times in a

20-year military career would it happen? I planned a full career. I was on my second enlistment. No part of my life was making sense to me.

I was a passionate, loving woman but had no one to love and no one to love me. I was 24 and a full-blown hypocrite. I was telling children to join the Navy. It's a time-honored organization of honor and duty and service. *Give up your life. Ladies you can give up your personal safety, your sense of security, self-esteem and trust in human nature. Please. Join us so you too can be raped or sexually violated at duty assignments everywhere around the world. It's not just an adventure. It's the Navy!*

It was noticed and commented upon by my peers and superiors that I had never enlisted a female. When I was asked to "close" on a potential female recruit my response was usually to the effect of, "Are you sure you're going to want me to tell her what she has to look forward to? What adventures await her when she least expects it?" My meaning and reputation were clear enough, but those dumb enough to have asked me only asked once.

With no hope of the future being any better than the past, I checked into Great Lakes Medical Center on **11 Nov 77.**

11 Nov 77 to 22 Feb 78 - Great Lakes Naval Medical Center

Diagnosed with Peptic Ulcer Disease and Anxiety on **24 Jan 78**, I was ordered into another clinical trial—this time for Cimetidine for ulcers. I almost immediately gained thirty pounds. I remember not minding the weight gain at all. My first reaction was—*Good! Nobody wants to fuck the fat girl.* No self-esteem left at all. I was broken. The hostile attitude noted by the nurse at Portsmouth Naval Hospital [so long ago] was completely absent. I didn't have a good fight left in me. There was nothing to get hostile about. I didn't want the Navy anymore. I didn't see it had anything to offer me so I had no fear of losing it. Any desperation to hold on to it was gone so I cared very little if it was about to be taken from me. So much for my Navy life. It was over.

I was put on convalescent leave and told to report once or twice a week. I had to drive from Lombard to Great Lakes in Waukegan. It was about a two-hour commute if the snow didn't double the drive. My Navy doctor said I was a high blood pressure shipwreck and had my ulcer raging by the time I got there after just my first few commutes. He put me on full convalescent leave to remain in my home in Lombard. I had to phone in muster at 0800 each day and report in person when ordered to do so. I was never again so ordered until late March 1978 for processing for discharge.

My medical records from Great Lakes Naval Medical Center are comprehensive. I was assigned to TPU (Transient Processing Unit) on **22 Feb 78**.

I was discharged from the Navy on **30 Mar 78** with Peptic Ulcer Disease and Anxiety Disorder—the old Navy fallback label for *'She can't take the sexual harassment and victimization.'* Code for *'We're done with her; get her out of here.'*

I was given Medical Severance Disability Pay.

I was directed to report to Base Legal to process out with a full Honorable Discharge.

I reported as ordered to Base Legal **30 Mar 78** where the eighth and final sexual incident of my five years took place. By then it mattered little to me. The worst had been done. The Military Sexual Trauma I had endured and its cumulative effect had destroyed my dream of a Navy career, shattering my trust in human nature and any feeling of personal safety I'd once known.

Incident #8

30 Mar 78 - Great Lakes Base Legal

While I was assigned to TPU (Transient Processing Unit) on **22 Feb 78** with my discharge date of **30 Mar 78,** I was awarded an Honorable Discharge under the medical diagnosis of Peptic Ulcer Disease and Anxiety Disorder, with Medical Severance Disability Pay.

30 Mar 78

As ordered, I reported to Great Lakes Base Legal at 0800 for discharge processing.

I was given a booklet in the JAG (Judge Advocate General's) office regarding my VA benefits registration. This is documented on my DD214. I signed it as directed.

Almost immediately upon signing, the Legalman sailors started offering to help me spend my severance pay. They spoke of how much better they could make me feel and what a quick and miraculous recovery I would make as soon as I had my money and my discharge in hand. It was said I would feel even better with one of them, or better all of them, in my bed. I tried one more time to reconcile in my head these ongoing patterns of behavior not just as single incidents or events but as the mores of a culture. I remembered thinking then—and really even more strongly now after documenting the MST I endured over the five years—it was never going to change. Not ever. There was such a sadness of finality to it.

I didn't even try to fend off their words. What amateurs they were with their sexual remarks and lewd suggestions. I remember thinking *Say what you will. I am done with you. You can't hurt me. I don't want this life anymore, and with that, you can't use it to hurt me anymore.* But they did hurt me. It didn't hurt any more than it ever had but it sure didn't hurt any less. My pain was not for sharing. It was all I had.

The Legalmen had given me the VA booklet as required in the discharge process, but upon the lack of my reaction and my lack of any signs of me being flattered by their offers, their taunts began in earnest. They were like a young pack of wolves learning to hunt as they circled their prey.

They were referencing my medical severance pay, saying how I wasn't really going to go to the VA because I had a tummy ache and was so sad about my failures as a sailor, was I?

They went on about the guys coming home from real service, missing limbs and suffering and *'you have a belly ache, a bad belly ache, a BIG Belly bad belly ache, a-look-at-the-size-of-that-belly kind of belly ache.'* (Recall I'd recently gained thirty pounds from the Cimetidine drug trial I was part of while in the care of Great Lakes Naval Hospital as stated in Incident #7.) So there it was again—the *nobody-likes-to-fuck-the-fat-girl* attitude. It was the parting shot, final validation of my worthlessness as a woman and a sailor. Right up to the last day of my service, MST was thriving. Any last-minute or lingering doubt I had about leaving the Navy was simply and irrevocably gone.

Regretfully, I never went to the VA although the military had recommended I receive 10% disability award for the rest of my life. I would've been getting benefits since 1978 for the diagnosis of Peptic Ulcer Disease. More importantly, I might have gotten the counseling to recover from the MST and the damage it carried into and throughout my life since. But I doubted it back then, so much so, I didn't even bother to check in with the VA when I was discharged.

MST wasn't validated back in the '70s. Any inability to handle the sexual pressure and ongoing harassment was dismissed but noted in one's military or medical records as anxiety disorders—bringing security clearance issues, preparedness doubts, and raising questions of mental health issues on the part of the female. Blame the victim. Praise the predator. Reward the bad behavior. The military still has much work to do to remedy the systemic nature of MST. The attitude in today's military is still *'in some incidents it is advisable to submit not resist'* [and] indicates how much work remains to be done. It is not unlike my brother's advice to "give it up; it's just a piece of ass, not worth getting hurt over." You can dress it up in political correctness; it's still a crass excuse for despicable acts.

I have been plagued with weight, digestive disorders, depression, and anxiety for much of my life. I have many letters from those close to me who have witnessed my efforts to overcome my struggles and input from professionals I have seen. I will make efforts to overcome.

I couldn't take it anymore; not one more interaction of sexual overtones. It was demoralizing. I was sure the VA would just be more of the same. I was conditioned to just not try anymore because every new effort or fresh beginning I'd given myself over the past five years in hopes of a different outcome had resulted in only more disappointment and spirit-breaking betrayal. I have wondered if the VA would have been the ones to redeem me but I never gave them the chance to show me I had value. I predetermined or prejudged how they would react. I wrote the VA off. I regret it.

Aftermath – directly following discharge

I shut down following my discharge. I slept away approximately the first 45 days in deep slumber about 20 hours of the day. If I didn't have to be awake or be somewhere then I just stayed in bed. I was more than sure the world wouldn't miss me. I slept it out. I felt like I was detoxing away the pain. When the dreams moved from nightmares of peril and loss into more vividly colorful pleasant escapes, I felt like I was feeling things again. I'd stopped drinking. Numbness I tried to wrap myself in no longer brought me the comfort it once had.

I had stopped dating because I reconnected with a wonderful man, a childhood friend. We got engaged in May 1978 and married in August 1978. We are still married 38 years later. I only recently shared with him what had really happened to me while in the Navy. He wrote a statement of how he feels it [has made an impact on] our [shared] life together. He is a Navy veteran as well. He had no idea of the depths of MST throughout the Navy. He defines his reaction as one of anger. He knew of my problems toward the end of my enlistment but not the full extent of how awful it was throughout my enlistment. There just wasn't a good time to tell him and so I just didn't. Like so much of what happened, I told myself I'd get back to it one day. (*and the little girl would be there, waiting for me.*)

I didn't want those five years to contaminate the future I hoped we had ahead of us. I tried to hold onto the good I had done and let go of the evil that was done to me. The little girl took on more promises of a day that would come but, for now, we had to keep it a secret. I knew in my heart, he was not the sort of man to follow his wife's career, although he would be supportive of my choices. I was even more certain he and I would have every chance at happiness if we put distance between the Navy and us.

Chapter Five
What's Happening Now

Now. You, the reader, have made it through THEN to NOW.

My NOW started the day in 2013 when I put in my retirement request from my profession as a DuPage County Sheriff's deputy, which commenced on July 3, 2014, I knew the THEN of my life was going to be very different, and NOW it is.

Every day prior to my retirement date on July 3, 2014, I had lived in a day-to-day life driven by the hopeful anticipation of NOW. However, my head was back in the THEN of my MST. THEN had pitched its stake in my heart. THEN drove my decisions, dictated my choices, undermined my happiness, and rotted my soul. But I didn't know how much THEN was controlling my life—I do know NOW.

NOW I'm ready to tell my story to all of you who suspected or questioned why I was so "different" after my time in the Navy. When I first came home back then, and in all the years that followed, I always felt I owed you an apology. I ask NOW that you accept this book as my apology.

"Now and then" can be a casual response to an innocuous question. "Now" and "then" are two words in need of reframing with the immediacy of life. I look at THEN as being as far in my past as my initial enlistment in the Navy in 1973. My NOW started in 2013.

I wasn't in a fog during all those years in between. Many of those years were good—even some of those years that I spent in the Navy. My husband, who I had known since we were in High School, and I came together just prior to my Honorable Discharge and were married three months later. My NOW years are even better than good. My love, our children, my joys all came into my life throughout those years. My very salvation is in the meaning they bring to my life.

NOW is upon me. NOW is authentic. NOW will have no secrets. NOW has nowhere to hide.

A big part of my awakening into the NOW of my MST came when I went searching through the VA website for medical benefit coverage as I was heading into retirement. On the VA website, in a sidebar box were the three letters "MST" that immediately caught my attention. *What's that?* I thought to myself. In a short page and a half, my life changed forever. As I read on, I could barely believe what I was seeing! Could this even be possible? NOW and at last, here was an authority ready to listen to what happened to me back THEN. An authority invested with the power to affect real change on behalf of those of us who had personally experienced the horrors of Military Sexual Trauma, as well as creating a vigilant watch for those yet to come. In that moment I came to know the time to tell my story had finally arrived.

From the Breton's Fisherman's Prayer (aka Seafarer's Poem) the words, "The sea, Oh God, so great, my boat so small," rose from the depths of my soul as I felt the little girl inside my mind and heart rise to the surface in the hope of fair winds and calm seas ahead.

MST is an experience. It is not a diagnosis. It is not a mental health condition. It is PTSD's ugly cousin. Suddenly, there was a burgeoning willingness in the health care profession and government bureaucracy to recognize this dimension of trauma as a devastating and debilitating experience, and address it in an assiduous manner.

Information for seeking help led me to the VetCenter. Apparently, there are multiple VetCenters in each state. As I read on, I was amazed to learn the level of confidentiality provided for the veteran. The veteran seeking help only need ask for the help, show the DD 214 (the one-page Department of Defense discharge certification) and help is provided. All treatment for physical and mental health conditions related to MST is free of charge. Services are available whether the attack or rape was reported back then or not. Veterans do not have to have a VA disability rating. The veteran can seek help by simply asking for it. No trips to the major medical VA hospitals. No voluminous paperwork or medical screenings demanded.

The red tape I had feared was more like a red velvet ribbon neatly wrapped around a box of creamy white chocolates.

My experience with the VA was as personally and uniquely my own as were the horrors I faced during my experiences of MST. As I share it with you here, please understand and recognize survivors will respond to treatment in a way that is unique to their own trauma. The point to be made—driven home like the tip of the saber—is that as painful as the inner confrontation may prove to be, it must take place for the journey of healing to begin. It has to happen when the survivor feels the time is right. Facing what we fear most allows us the grace of purpose not only to vanquish the enemy but also to triumph on all fronts.

Admittedly, I was suspicious from the beginning. I had found the VetCenter in late July 2014. I made my appointment. I canceled it almost as quickly. I called the VetCenter again. I talked with the MST counselor but still couldn't commit to keeping an appointment.

Why wasn't I ready to let go of the "THEN"? The answer and the help were before me NOW. I hadn't even done any of the paperwork to register at the VetCenter yet, but they were already making time for me. The little girl in my head was screaming *NOW, Diane! NOW! Why are you hesitating?* It took me many scheduled and canceled appointments before I could finally bring myself to keep an appointment in February 2015. Even with that, I put the MST counselor through the ringer to see if she was going to be any good at this. I wanted to make sure that she was going to be able to handle the level of intensity that had been building inside of me for such a long time when it came pouring out.

It was my time for questions and demands. I didn't make it easy for the MST counselor. I wanted to know if she was a veteran. If not, then how could she possibly understand the severity of MST? She was not a veteran. I made up my mind. She couldn't possibly understand. No. She had, however, been treating MST victims for over 20 years. *What?!*

Somewhat sheepishly, I admitted that *Okay, maybe I should give her a chance. She might really know what she's doing*. Today, I can confidently tell you that counselor (we'll call her "Dr. P") is an extraordinary woman.

I was tentative for the first few weeks, but "Dr. P" was patient. She was kind and compassionate while being a taskmaster nudging me along into the darkness. There were 40 years burying the five years we needed to get at. It was work. It was painful, but it was debriding the wounds. There were years of coping strategies to dismantle.

When I reminded her that she had said it was going to get better if we kept at it, "Dr. P" informed me it was going to get a lot worse before it got any better. We laughed—actually laughed. "Oh you failed to mention that," I responded.

How did I get to a place where my MST journey could cause me to laugh aloud? I got there through the VetCenter every Wednesday morning at 8:00 a.m.

Each Wednesday morning as I headed out on the 45-minute trip to my appointment, I had and still do have the hesitation pit-in-my-stomach feeling. I have tried to tell myself I don't really need it, that I worked my way through a very good life all these years without counseling. I could just continue to keep it to myself and no one need ever know. All this going on in my head as I continue to drive to my appointments, because I know at my very core that I did and do still need it.

Early on, sessions were twice a week. Was I building the habit of showing up, or had my counselor seen what a powder keg. I was? It wasn't until about four months in, when I realized I was looking forward to the weekly ripping open of old wounds. A short time later, "Dr. P" gave me two incredible gifts. First, she shared with me a story of a monthly conference telephone call she shared with other psychoanalysts who treated MST victims. She told me she had shared my case characteristics and components (as we previously agreed she might do one day) among the other professionals—their purpose being the sharing of collective minds, wisdom and experience generating methodologies and insights to the mutual benefit of their clients. It's not like they all had jobs where they can go home and chat it up with the neighbors about their day in the office and gather advice from others in how to handle their daily routines. As "Dr. P" spoke of me, a Detroit doctor interrupted to inquire for more specifics. It seems she also had a Navy WAVE, approximately the same age, same backstory of the delayed reporting, same cycle of ongoing MST spanning years and multiple duty stations. The Detroit doctor had serious concerns that she and "Dr. P" were treating the very same WAVE.

The similarities were just that strong, right down to the time-stamp of the stay in Portsmouth for the clinical trial. It took some further clarification before they had the revelation that if this had happened to two of us, it must certainly have happened to more. There it was—the gift of validation! It hadn't just happened to me!

An ongoing pattern of deceitful collaboration between the military and medical profession was identified as clearly well practiced, perfected, and pervasive.

It was then that "Dr. P" gave me the second gift. She said there was a documentary she believed I was now strong enough to be able to watch. It was the gift of knowledge, a confirmation of my ownership of the Military Sexual Trauma. She loaned me her copy. I took it home and stared at it for days before I believed I was strong enough to watch it. I watched it alone and I wept. I've now shared it with 46 other people. It never gets easier to watch. It does fortify my resolve to continue to heal.

I had entered the military with a perspective of innocence and expectation. This was all I wanted as a young naïve girl. Most anyone that knew me prior to the military viewed me as streetwise and somewhat clever; but that was clearly in the context of a small Midwestern town, not what awaited me in the Navy.

Only now do I have the realization I was never alone in this. Others tirelessly fought the battle from their level. A good war well fought comes at the enemy from multifaceted strategies of attack. So it is with MST. We must all become warriors—NOW—attacking from all angles while tending to our wounded.

I want to tell you a bit about the documentary. I wholeheartedly endorse it. I hope you buy it and share it with as many people as you can.

To the naysayers insisting that nobody's going to want to know this or would want to see this, I say, *So what? Be bold. Be daring enough to bring this topic out of the darkness so we can bring this plague to an end.*

Written and directed by Academy Award-nominated director, Kirby Dick, the documentary ***The Invisible War*** won the Audience Award at the Sundance Film Festival in 2012. It was also the New York Times Critics Pick as one of the ten best movies of 2012.

In this investigative documentary, the epidemic of rape within our Armed Forces is exposed, and the facts are supported by Department of Defense statistics. The level of betrayal is underscored by the fact that today "a female soldier in a combat zone is more likely to be raped by a fellow soldier than killed by enemy fire." Go buy this video and get as many good people to watch it as you can.

I now keep my Wednesday appointments unless otherwise rescheduled by the counselor. Regrettably, after working with "Dr. P" for ten months, she had to relocate to an area near Eglin Air Force Base in Florida—our loss, their incredible gain. She left me in good hands when she turned my case over to Counselor "L". "Dr. P" had taken me to the edge, shared my growth, and her style of therapy was a gift toward my restoration.

Counselor "L" introduced a new way of attacking my trauma. She is not "Dr. P". Her methods are not "Dr. P's". With Counselor "L", the challenge began from a new vector, a new trajectory, a new perspective. I was afraid all over again. "Dr. P" understood me. We'd established a rhythm. I didn't feel abandoned, but I was apprehensive of what Counselor "L" would bring to my journey.

I was too quick to let myself believe Counselor "L" wasn't going to be a good fit for where I wanted my therapy to go. The first three or four appointments were confusing, at best. Oddly, I found myself intrigued by her approach, which was, "Where is my life now, and how will I function now?" She assured me that in time we would revisit what happened back then, but she was adamant that I give her way a fair chance. I was surprised by my initial acceptance of Counselor "L" and my willingness to relinquish any resistance to follow her, when normally I would have reacted just the opposite.

In truth, Counselor "L" exhausts me in a way I am not fully able to explain. It's good. I feel it's really good. In ten months together so far, it's clear that we've only scratched the surface. Mere thoughts of what lies ahead have me feeling somewhat drained but looking forward to it.

If you know me at all (and I feel you do by this point in the book) then you know I do not like to be controlled. I like to be in control. I don't easily give up control. Yet, here I am willingly letting Counselor "L" drive my therapy.

The sessions are intense (as were those with "Dr. P") and bewildering, but no more so than being spent and bewildered by my MST. I'm not always sure how each counseling session will turn out week to week, but I'm looking forward to each one. The entire process is stirring up the emotional side of the MST while giving me newer and healthier ways of sorting it all out.

Counselor "L" says we will reach back into the trauma by titrating the treatment. I never heard the word before but the analogy is so spot-on to what's needed to help me reframe my MST experience. There is work to do, and although "Counselor "L" is not "Dr. P", "Counselor "L" is exactly what I need right now.

Moving further into my present-day life, I'm able to put the trauma into context. Where it happened and at the will of another has to be given the weight it deserves. Violation of trust works in direct opposition to the military environment's every effort to build self-reliance in balance with camaraderie. There are still accounts I need to reconcile.

I wish I could admit to fantasies of torturous acts of revenge or eternal damnation of my attackers. I never had any of those. I couldn't get past my own pain to be wishing or envisioning them rotting in hell. Not even my nightmares give me the satisfaction. I can only work on getting my MST to a tolerable place in my life.

I see the MST for the life-changing event it was when it happened. Looking back on the nearly 40 years of keeping it to myself, I notice how it affected my health and my quality of life. Still, it's been a great life. I did better than just function or just get by, but I recognize I was among the fortunate few. The love of my family was paramount in my journey.

I also recognize certain reactions I had to certain events. I know my intensity and tenacity are offshoots of my MST. The hypervigilance, suspiciousness, strong emotions and control issues—what might otherwise be considered to be negative traits—ultimately made me a better than average cop. I came out of the Navy with an unexpected skill set. It served me well in an unexpected manner.

What happened to me has to have meaning. I'm aware of why I have ongoing bouts of sleeplessness or vivid nightmares. I am aware of why I am jumpy, why I have an exaggerated startle response and feel unsafe in crowds. I'm not just "drifty" or "forgetful" or "flighty"—there's a reason for each of these. Finally, I make sense to me. I'm flawed. I'm damaged but not defeated. I have difficulties. Who doesn't? I have the blessing of knowing the origin.

I've been given the gift of sorting through "why I am how I am" and having caring professionals and loving friends and family helping me get it sorted. At long last, the traumatic incidents have meaning. The impact of MST is at the root of so many other sufferings in my life since—not just my own, but those who love me and have unknowingly shared in my struggles and pain through the fallout. I've discovered how important it is to work toward my healing not just for myself but for all those I love and who love me.

I want the journey to have more meaning. It has to matter to everyone. It does affect everyone. It has to stop.

Chapter Six
Who? When? How?

As much as I might caution my readers to prepare themselves for the revelation of this brutal truth, I was giving very deliberate thought to who I would first expose to the raw details of my MST. I had been in counseling for more than six months. My family all knew it was for "some crap that happened to me in the Navy that needs to be sorted out." It was enough of an explanation at first. It was like telling your kids about sex—just enough to answer the question you thought they might have, but not so much as to confuse them or harm them.

I was piecemealing my snapshot memories. I was watching for signs or cues from them to try to determine how much more they might be ready to know. I held the reins tightly.

Our daughter, Heather. Mothers and daughters have a special language, a way of communicating that is not always verbal. Heather is a gifted empath. She knew I was gauging and watching and waiting. Over the years of her upbringing, our arguing skills often went from bantering to outright bitching while our guys stood in amazement or intervened to get peace. Throughout those same years, we had developed skills whereby we could short-circuit a topic to bring it to a sudden close or call each other out from their hiding place. Heather was the first to enact this ploy by calling me out on my spoon-feeding of information. In the nicest of ways, she demanded I tell her every last bit of it; all the horrific attacks, the sadness and the trauma.

Heather wanted a full disclosure of where I was with all of it right now at this point and whom I had told. I whispered to her, "Only you baby girl, only you." And in that moment the mother became the child. My words to her throughout her childhood, through her traumas of adolescence and heartbreaks were lovingly echoed back by her to comfort me.

When I told my sweet, strong daughter what a good

Mum she had become, she smiled and said, "I learned from the best." And we laughed.

It was agreed that I needed to unburden myself of the load I had carried too long alone. I still didn't know how to tell my Leos (the strong, loving, authentic gentlemen in my life who all happened to have been born under the zodiac sign of Leo.) These lion-hearted leaders of goodness and compassion graced my life each day and are deeply loved in my heart. I just couldn't find the words to tell them yet, so I gave myself permission to forestall, at least for the time being.

My redheaded superhero squadron was another matter entirely. These are the females in my life by birth or by blessing who have red hair (gingers) by birth or by bottle. They know who they are, as does anyone who observes the strength and love they bring to my life. I am blessed beyond measure to have their love and support. They have my back and I have theirs. Just as in the case of my Leos full disclosure was not yet comfortably forthcoming, so I gave myself permission to forestall with them as well for the time being.

The gift of my journey has blessed me with an unexpected and delightful international addition to my redheaded superhero gang. She is all of 13 years old and has the spirit of a wood sprite. In our daughter's marriage to a scouser in Liverpool, my little sprite and I became loosely related. This joyful child embodies the innocence of childhood and the optimism for what is yet to be. She bears a startling similarity to the little girl inside me to whom I'd made so many promises. My wish for this little redheaded superhero is that she may never experience such trauma as I have known in this life. May I have the joy to relive my days of childhood wonder by watching her thrive.

My intention was always to protect those I love most dearly. Sharing guardedly, I was not withholding out of selfishness. I would have to tell my husband, Michael. I searched my heart for a way to inform him while protecting him at the same time. His love and support of my Wednesday morning appointments is a priority. He was tuned into my struggle and he deserved a better insight than I'd provided for him in the past. He never pried or prodded or pushed.

By the time I'd decided to divulge to him my long-kept private terrors we had been married well over 35 years. I had protected him as long as I could. Michael was aware that I'd been given a copy of *The Invisible War*. I told him I had watched it and it was impactful. I asked if perhaps sometime he would want to watch it with me because I wanted to watch it again—but not *alone* ever again. Always supportive and loving, Michael agreed, "Sure we could."

I admit I was concerned how he would handle the subject matter. This concern stemmed from my solid belief in him as a man of good character and integrity. Never could he have possibly known of the horrors of MST and how it permeated our Navy. In my sharing of the documentary with him, my belief was confirmed. Michael was horrified and said he was "ashamed" of this behavior among the ranks. *Oh, my dear, sweet Michael.*

After viewing the documentary, as we sat on the couch somewhat numb from what we had just seen, he looked at me with his big brown fudge-ball eyes that I still to this day get lost in, and asked, "Is this anything like what happened to you?" I could only nod in confirmation as my eyes welled up with tears. I could find no words to soften the blow.

As gently as I could I asked him, "Do you think you might be ready to hear about it?"

He said, "Only if you're ready to tell me."

I knew if I started to tell him any of it, I would be telling him all of it. I cautioned him that we could stop at any point and come back to it again another time. I think he knew at that moment, although we didn't talk about it specifically, I had fallen victim to MST more than once.

For the next four and a half hours, we sat on the couch sharing the burden of the secret I had kept through our entire marriage. We talked. We cried, but as with so many things we had faced together in life we would face this together as well. When it was all said and there was nothing more to tell, I found myself wondering why I had waited so long. What had I expected to happen? As if he had heard my thoughts, Michael commented, "Did you think I was going to go *POOF!* and disappear? You are mine and I am yours, and we will do this together. Going forward into whatever happens now, we will face it together."

Michael knew I was in counseling with the VA. He knew I had worked diligently in filing a claim for disability and he had been supportive throughout that process. He knew it made me feel validated when the VA awarded me my disability entitlement. Michael knew I had resubmitted my paperwork with Social Security and their decision to deem me permanently and totally disabled further validated the authenticity of the damage done by MST.

I told Michael I thought I might want to write a book about my experience so that maybe I could warn other unsuspecting young women of the potential dangers awaiting them in the military. I would want to write it in a way that would encourage them to serve their country while not allowing the flaws of the system to rob them of the honor and dignity of being in the armed forces.

I felt the story needed to be told by someone with direct personal knowledge who was wounded and somewhat broken by the experience but still able to serve her country just as any woman should be able. I wanted the book to inspire the strong young women of our country to prevail, serve, and surpass the obstacles placed before them. Forewarned is forearmed.

It was not at all surprising to me that my amazing husband supported me in my decision 100%. Among the many moments related to the military where I can find cause for regret, one of the single biggest is that I hadn't told Michael so many years ago. Even still, we have a marriage stronger than most, blessed beyond measure with enough love to last a lifetime.

Our son, my miracle, Evan. Was I ever going to be able to tell him? I had wanted to wait to tell him until I could show the facts and the validation and certifications of the VA and Social Security. The delay felt foolish to me. On the one hand, I wanted to be able to prove to him that what I was saying was true. On the other hand, how ridiculous was this posture? My son would require no proof. My words held all the veracity and belief he ever needed. It was a stipulation I had manufactured in my head. I had embedded some ludicrous notion that these documents would make the truth more truthful. It was absurd. It was unnecessary. It was a lame excuse I fabricated to rationalize not telling him. He is such a good man, my son. There is a fine line between protecting those we love and fearing the loss of their love and respect.

I refer to Evan as my miracle because the Navy left me with a reasonable degree of certainty I would not be able to have children following the ravaging rendered upon me in Portsmouth Naval Hospital. I had suffered two miscarriages early in my life with Michael. It reaffirmed for me that I would be punished for all time by never knowing motherhood. My belief that this would be the case was erased by the blessed birth of Evan, my miracle. In fact, Evan had a difficult arrival. I had to come home from the hospital without him and wait a worry-filled week before his health had stabilized to bring him home. In a moment of clarity, I saw this as another reminder of how close I came to never knowing the joy of having Evan.

Now that I decided I would write a book, the obligation to Evan was as much of respect as it was of morality. I asked if he and I might talk some Sunday for a few hours as I had some things I wanted to share with him. Not because I felt I owed it to him but because I love him. Anyone who knows me, moreover, anyone who knows Evan, knows he is a gentleman from a bygone era. He is an old soul in a simple man. He is truly one of my favorite people on earth.

This Leo to whom I'd given birth embodies all that is good. How was I ever going to tell him? We set a date for the Sunday we would get together. The telling was nearly six hours. I won't share what was said or how it was said because it was a mother-son moment for our shared memory alone. There should never have been any hesitation on my part to tell him. It's done. It's sorted. Enough said.

Chapter Seven
A Word about Clichés

Clichés. Clichés get to be clichés by being true. Clichés are often used as weaponry spoken by the sender trying to make their point as succinctly as possible while disarming the receiver with the accuracy of a well-crafted word or phrase. Clichés often leave the sender feeling victorious and the receiver feeling defeated.

Clichés have a way of sticking with us. Spoken words ring true where the written word can often fall short of the mark, lacking the sting of emphasis. Does saying it aloud help us to believe? Who among us hasn't replayed a volleyed cliché repeatedly in his or her head?

Although I've never heard them from the people close to me, in my head I imagine certain clichés ring true creating a deafening barrage of emotional assaults. The imagined sting is no less real and no less wounding.

What follows is a list of clichés I imagined I would surely have heard had I told anyone about what happened during my five years in the Navy. I wasn't ready to hear them aloud when my wounds were so fresh. I am ready to hear these clichés now.

"It's in the past, let it go."
"It's not as bad as all that."
"Get over it. Get over yourself."
"Don't think about it. Put it behind you."
"It isn't who you are; it's just something that happened to you."
"Don't let it define you."
"You did nothing wrong. Don't blame yourself."
"Time heals all wounds."
"They can't hurt you anymore."
"Just have a good cry and move on."
"Give it some time. You'll forget." (40 years later might suggest otherwise.)
"It won't always hurt this bad."

It all sounds somewhat trite when you see all those clichés together. Worse than those are the clichés that take on an accusatory tone. Someone who has little regard for the person they are speaking to or their pain, use these hurtful clichés all too frequently.

"Whose fault is it, if it's not yours?"
"You asked for it."
"It can't be undone."
"We all have our crosses to bear in life."
"You've only yourself to blame."
"This is why nice girls don't go into the military."
"Military women should expect this."
"You're the one who wanted to go in the military. What did you think was going to happen?"
"Men in the military only want women there for one thing."

The last four of these clichés particularly grate on me. I actually did hear a few of them spoken in some form—sometimes to me and sometimes in snippets of conversations I overheard between others. I caution anyone who would like to comment on anyone's military service or Military Sexual Trauma to tread softly and be gentle with the words you speak.

No woman who chooses to serve her country with honor and dignity should ever, by anyone—male or female—have her autonomy brought into question by anyone else. I find the last cliché to be equally insulting to the quality of the men who serve in our military. Any of these clichés, if spoken to me before I began my healing journey out of MST, would have been met with a cross response and a most polite invitation to go to hell, though with what Irish diplomacy I could muster I would have had you looking forward to the trip.

Today, it's an opportunity for both of us to learn. I may bristle but we both will live.

Chapter Eight
Getting Over MST is Like Being at a Funeral

etting over Military Sexual Trauma (MST) is similar to going to a funeral. As the bereaved family stands there, people pass by paying their respects and feeling the need to say something comforting or kind. Enter the moment where clichés come to life. "I'm sorry for your loss." Say it aloud if it will help you believe it.

The bereaved family must graciously listen—not necessarily wanting to hear it, but allowing this ritual of paying respects and the formality of those attending the funeral to say the very things the family doesn't want to hear.

Every attempt and well-intentioned, kindly worded cliché is another platitude and acknowledgment of the heart-wrenching event that has brought everyone together. Someone has died and so it is with rape. The biggest difference being that death has finality to it for the victim and the survivors.

Rape (sexual assault/unlawful restraint/aggravated sexual battery) has no such reprieve. There is some finality, but it is also a recurring death—the death of innocence, the death of sense of self, of trust and of loss, and so much more, and is ongoing. As though absolutely gutted of all emotion, intimacy becomes a dark abstract of what it once was. Often in a sexually intimate scenario, the sexual act itself becomes an effort to make sense of past assaults, to seek a new understanding, and to rediscover the joy in making love with a safe and caring partner.

Searching to reconcile the cumulative effect of those five years only yielded fragments and fractions of who I was. The sum total of these fractions of an existence didn't equal a complete life; not the life I had before MST.

I always knew I was alone in this, yet she (the little girl inside my head) was always with me and still is. For her own well-being, she's still keeping care that she wasn't or isn't destroyed by all we endured throughout those years. As for the years since, there is a sorrow to the repeating questions in my head . . . *What would you have had me do differently back then?* and *What would you have me do now?* It can't be undone.

Funerals. This is another reason I don't attend them anymore. Those I might have considered attending in the past and didn't, and those I might consider or be asked by others to consider attending in the future, just know that I won't be going. The deceased, past or future, will have known their place in my life and mine in theirs. The ritual and the ceremony of attending funerals and offering my respects to the bereaved simply will no longer happen. The aftermath of death and its finality has my respect. MST has no such finality.

WITH GRATITUDE

With gratitude, I appreciate how life has brought me to a place where I can revisit what happened to me while I was in the US Navy. I feel I can now look back, not with forgiveness—for what they did was unforgivable—but with the perspective provided by time and distance, I can really examine what happened back then under the umbrella of the protection of my life as it is in the present.

With gratitude, I can now reflect upon my life. While in the midst of MST, I had so many questions needing answers yet so many answers I questioned. It is with gratitude I now see how a life pattern began to establish itself in my psyche, and become ingrained in my constant discontent and mistrust.

With gratitude for my guardian angels who, although they could not protect me from the attacks, kept me from any lasting physical harm. So many victims of MST suffer horrible episodes of violent physical attacks. It is with gratitude I realize I was spared any physically visible scars.

With gratitude for my broken heart in Cuba. I learned through my encounter with "D's" wife that my broken heart was a blessing, lest I could have actually ended up married to and stuck on a backwoods farm in the hills of West Virginia with such a poor excuse of a man.

With gratitude for those in authority who had me stationed with my brother through most of my military career. Although he was probably not as aware as I was of the stabilizing effect he had on the chaos of my life during the times of the attacks, he was my rock.

With gratitude, I appreciate the good and decent men such as CDR Alvin Marsh and ADM "B" who demonstrated during each day of their service that honor and integrity still mattered.

With gratitude for my loving husband, Michael, and our beautiful children, for without them life would have no meaning.

With gratitude, I acknowledge how the values instilled within me during my upbringing did not allow for quitting on our country, regardless of the tragedies I lived through while I served. With absolute gratitude to have served our country with honor. I would again. I would encourage every woman to exercise her right to do so.

With gratitude, deepest appreciation, and the most heartfelt thank you to you, my readers, for considering what I've written here and what I went through to bring you my story. My journey and the path I must now take to address the Military Sexual Trauma I endured now calls upon me, and perhaps you as well, to take my experiences forward by sharing this book with others who still search the darkness trying to find their way through the daunting and haunting specter of MST.

With my deepest gratitude.

Diane (Madden) Ferguson

ABOUT THE AUTHOR

Diane Madden Ferguson is a US Navy veteran and retired law enforcement officer. She is a graduate of Benedictine University with a Master's of Science in Management and Organizational Behavior.

Undertow is Diane's first book. Her paper on "Gender Specific Stress in Law Enforcement" was published in the Western Illinois University Online Law Journal's very first issue in 2010.

Diane's personal experience with MST compels her to share her journey in a mission of caution and comfort to those serving in our military. It is her hope and intention with this memoir and her website to create a platform to enact change and create awareness of the magnitude of this pervasive issue within the military culture.

Diane has now been married for 38 years and living in the western suburbs of Chicago where she has been blessed to raise a family with her husband, Michael. With all children now grown adults, Diane and Michael cherish the comfort and companionship of each other and their Boston Terrier, Mercy.

Her favorite pastime is enjoying the company of her grandson, Owen, as often as possible—whether on Skype or traveling to see him in person where he lives in Liverpool, England. She also enjoys DIY television and creative projects that involve repurposing trash to treasures.

As a writer and now published author, Diane herself is truly a literary treasure and so much more!

Visit her website at www.UndertowTheBook.com

Made in the USA
Columbia, SC
23 June 2018